IMPACT OF PARTITION: REFUGEES IN PAKISTAN

The Regional Centre for Strategic Studies (RCSS) is an independent, non-profit and non-governmental organization for collaborative research, networking and interaction on strategic and international issues pertaining to South Asia. Set up in 1992, the RCSS is based in Colombo, Sri Lanka.

The RCSS is a South Asian forum for studies, training and multi-track dialogue and deliberation on issues of regional interest. All activities of RCSS are designed with a South Asia focus and are usually participated by experts from all South Asian countries. The Centre is envisaged as a forum for advancing the cause of co-operation, security, conflict resolution, confidence building, peace and development in the countries of the South Asian region.

The RCSS serves its South Asian and international constituency by: (a) networking programmes that promote interaction, communication and exchange between institutions and individuals within and outside the region engaged in South Asian strategic studies; (b) organizing regional workshops and seminars and sponsoring and coordinating collaborative research-, and (c) disseminating output of the research through publications which include books, monographs and a quarterly newsletter. The RCSS facilitates scholars and other professionals of South Asia to address, mutually and collectively, problems and, issues of topical interest for all countries of the region.

Queries may be addressed to:

Regional Centre for Strategic Studies
2 Elibank Road
Colombo 5
SRI LANKA
Tel: (94-11) 2599734, 599735
Fax: 2599993; e-mail: edrcss@sri.lanka.net
RCSS website: http://www.rcss.org

RCSS Policy Studies 37

IMPACT OF PARTITION: REFUGEES IN PAKISTAN

Struggle for Empowerment and State's Response

AMTUL HASSAN

REGIONAL CENTRE FOR STRATEGIC STUDIES
COLOMBO

MANOHAR
2006

Published by
Ajay Kumar Jain for
Manohar Publishers & Distributors
4753/23 Ansari Road, Daryaganj
New Delhi 110 002
and
Regional Centre for Strategic Studies
2 Elibank Road
Colombo 5
SRI LANKA
Tel: (94-11) 2599734-5; Fax: 2599993;
e-mail: edrcss@sri.lanka.net
Website: http://www.rcss.org

First published 2006

Views expressed in materials published in RCSS Policy Studies are of contributors, and not necessarily of the Regional Centre for Strategic Studies

ISBN 81-7304-698-0

Printed at
Lordson Publishers Pvt Ltd
Delhi 110 007

Distributed in South Asia by
FOUNDATION BOOKS
4381/4, Ansari Road
Daryaganj, New Delhi 110 002
and its branches at Mumbai, Hyderabad,
Bangalore, Chennai, Kolkata

To my beloved
and most respected parents,
whose support made me able
to complete this book

Contents

RCSS is grateful to the
Ford Foundation for its generous
support for the Kodikara Award
on which this report is based.

Acknowledgements

I am grateful to God for providing me this opportunity of researching and writing this paper for the Regional Centre for Strategic Studies (RCSS), Colombo, Sri Lanka. I am deeply thankful from the core of heart to my great teacher, Professor Sikander Mehdi of the International Relations Department, University of Karachi, whose guidance from the first word till the end has been a boon to me. He examined my Kodikara Award project, and encouraged me to accomplish my task. His help and suggestions in this regard will always be remembered. Many thanks are due to the Librarian and Staff, Pakistan Institute of International Affairs, Karachi; Area Study Center for Europe, University of Karachi; and the Pakistan Study Center, University of Karachi, specially Anwar-ul-Haq, Afsar Mehdi, Zameer Ahmed, Abdul Hameed and Aziz Ahmed for providing the necessary assistance and facilities for collecting data and other relevant material for this project.

I have benefited from the highly entertaining, rational and challenging conversations with scholars, journalists, intellectuals and former diplomats, specially former Foreign Minister, Major General Sahabzada Yaqub Khan (Retd.), (Member of the National Assembly), Haider Abbas Rizvi (MQM), Arshad Hasan (Deputy Registrar, Nadirshaw Edulji Dinshaw University), Dr Sabiha H. Syed, Dr Aliya Imam, Dr Imtiaz H. Bokhari, Dr Pervaiz Iqbal Cheema, Dr Noor-ul-Haq, Lieutenant General Kamal Matinuddin (Retd.), A. H. Nayyar, Liaquat Banori, Saleem Shah, Asma Shakir, Dr Ijaz Hussain, Dr Mohammad Waseem, Dr Tariq Rehman, Dr Sikander Hayyat, Dr Noman Sattar, Dr Rasheed Ahmed, Dr Mubarak Ali, Ahmed Salim, Kazim Imam, Shafquat Munir, Husain Naqi, Khawaja A. Jaweed, Riaz Mehdi, Abida Mehmood, S. Mohammed Mehdi

Rizvi, Usman Qureshi, Mrs and Mr Mansoor Raza, Jaffer Mehdi, Muhammad Tariq and Shafi Adabi, with whom I discussed the theme of my research. Their comments and views on various aspects of my research project have been quite valuable.

Nusrat Khurshedi, Ph.D. student in the Department of International Relations, University of Karachi, Ishtiaq Ali Mehkri, journalist, *Dawn* (Karachi), and Ali Imtiaz, journalist, *News*, helped me search for relevant sources for this project. I am thankful for their cooperation. I am also grateful to Hasan Abbas, who typed the manuscript diligently.

In the end, I owe thanks to my family members, especially my parents, whose moral support proved to be essential for the successful completion of this research project.

June 2005 AMTUL HASSAN

Introduction

Human beings have always been moving from place to place. Sometimes they moved in small numbers, but often in large groups. They moved with members of their own families, in large groups of several families, or of members of the same clan, tribe, ethnic, or religious community. Their travels were voluntary or involuntary, directed to seeking a better future, greener pastures, security, and dignity.

During the last decade of the twentieth century, governments, international organizations and the public have become increasingly aware of the problems faced by refugees and internally displaced people. The problem of forced displacement, however, is not new. Neither are international efforts to alleviate the sufferings of such people, but the fact is that the international community has not fully succeeded in combating prejudice, persecution, poverty and other root causes of conflicts and displacement. Throughout history, people have had to abandon their homes and seek safety elsewhere to escape persecution, armed conflicts, or political violence. This has happened in different regions of the world, and millions have had to flee their homes.

But the movement of people in the twentieth century through the length and breadth of Asia, Africa, South America, Central America, Europe and North America is unprecedented in the history of migration, gigantic in scale, and often very tragic. Most, as it was, were victims of circumstance, misgovernance, war, conflict, violence, and ethnic campaigns. These were people plucked from their native environs and forced to flee. They ultimately formed part of transferred populations. Primarily the issue of international displacement did not feature prominently on international agenda.

However, when the League of Nations was formed, the refugee problem was given due attention. After the Second World War, the UN focussed on the issue of post-War displacements. Soon after, the UNHCR and UNRWA were established and they dealt with numerous refugee situations. The UNHCR in particular was concerned with the flight of people from the former European colonies in Asia and Africa. In the long drawn out Algerian war of Independence, the widespread use of torture by the French forces provoked many Algerians to flee the country. They took refuge in Tunisia and Morocco in the late 1950s and early 1960s. According to a UNHCR report some 30,000 people had fled the country within the short span of two years. Similarly, after the breakup of former Yugoslavia and dissolution of the Soviet Union and Czechoslovakia, millions of people were forced to flee their home. Moreover, after the genocide in Rawanda in 1994, over two million Rwandans fled to Zaire, Tanzania, Burandi and Uganda. According to a UNHCR report 2,50,000 Rwandans fled to Tanzania in 24 hours. But in the case of South Asia, the Partition of 1947, described as the largest migration of people in human history and memory, involved over ten million people from India and Pakistan.

The people migrating from the territories now comprising Pakistan and settling down in India and those fleeing from East Punjab, the United Provinces (UP, now Uttar Pradesh), the Central Provinces (now MP, Madhya Pradesh), Bihar and West Bengal to the two provinces of Pakistan, East Pakistan (now Bangladesh) and West Pakistan (present-day Pakistan), constitute a large part of the transferred populations of the twentieth century. Much of this migration took place in the wake of violence, killing, and abduction.

A radical shift in the population took place on the eve of Pakistan's Independence, and the bulk of migration occurred in the four months between August and November 1947 and soon after. Two kinds of migration have continued to change the demographic realities in Sind and Punjab. The urban areas in the two provinces became centres of refugee concentration. Lahore and Karachi became huge population centres overnight. The process began with Partition, when the worst kind of communal riots, especially in the Punjab, resulted in a holocaust. The massive exchange of populations between both the countries affected both Pakistani Punjab and the Sind province.

Managing the refugees was not an easy task for Pakistan. It was a great challenge for a state which had just been created and had to begin from scratch. Indeed, the task of looking after the millions of refugees streaming in from diverse directions, providing shelter to them, and arranging for food and medical services was not an easy task.

The newly created country was in chaos. Its treasury was empty. It didn't have organized civic structures, and there was violence, uncertainty, and gloom. But Pakistan, under the leadership of its first Governor-General, Mohammed Ali Jinnah and Prime Minister, Liaquat Ali Khan did not shy away from its responsibilities to the incoming refugees from India.

Pakistan had to create space for the waves of incoming refugees, establish camps in different areas and reserve localities evacuated by the departing non-Muslims for the incoming Muslim population. It also faced a lot of problems in providing food supplies to the refugee camps. The transport facilities were inadequate, medical aid was not adequately available, and there were worries regarding the safety of the refugees. However, Pakistan tried to deal with the complex issues as effectively as it could.

In fact, the whole issue of rehabilitation and resettlement was affected through the distribution of evacuee property and governmental assistance programme which followed after providing immediate relief to the refugees at the receiving points and in camps. Next to be taken up was the issue of defining the legal status of these refugees, and the formalization of a comprehensive agreement with India over evacuee property, citizenship, and visits of refugees to their relatives and family members left behind. Soon to be addressed was the issue of reintegration of the refugees with society and their involvement in the political and electoral networks and systems.

Thus, in about a decade or so after the creation of Pakistan, i.e. from August 1947 to October 1958, which saw the rise and fall of a series of governments, Pakistan systematically dealt with the numerous issues relating to refugee management. In Sind, the local

Sindhis welcomed the influx of the Partition refugees (mainly Urdu-speaking people from north India). The locals came forward to share food and clothing with them, assist them and readily underwent hardships for the sake of rehabilitating them. They were gradually integrated into the new state and empowered. They played important roles in politics, programmes of economic development and the military. They joined the bureaucracy, judiciary, police, Armed Forces, business, and the emerging civil society. Many came from very advanced centres of learning, politics and civil society in India, and they asserted themselves.

Migration created two types of refugees. First, there were the refugees from East Punjab, who had migrated and settled mostly in West Punjab. Owing to the shared language and culture, the Punjabi immigrants assimilated themselves quickly in West Punjab, ceased to identify themselves as Muhajirs and integrated themselves in the new land. Second, the refugees who came from UP, CP, and elsewhere in northern India decided to move to Sind: they felt comfortable about identifying themselves as *Muhajireen* and were hesitant in identifying themselves as 'Sindhis' or 'New Sindhis'. In Sind, the refugees were not fully entertained by the State, and every successive government treated them as a pawn. When they expressed fear and uncertainty about their future and raised questions regarding their rights, the state remained reluctant to accept their demands. It assumed unnecessary, painful and coercive measures to suppress their aspirations which eventually led to ethnic tension in Sind, and the refugees began to review their attitudes towards the State. Ethnic strife became increasingly explosive in the absence of a political platform.

Fissures began to appear soon enough. The post-Partition euphoria was not to last long. The tussle for power and favour between locals and non-locals began, and with the advent of the military regime of Ayub Khan (1958–69), the power and influence of the Partition refugees was systematically curtailed. Worst affected was the city of Karachi, then the capital city of united Pakistan, which had become the city of Partition refugees. The capital was shifted to Islamabad during Ayub's time, and business families of West Pakistan were encouraged to shift their business headquarters there. Employment opportunities for the refugees shrank and the reign of discrimination began. The Yahya Government also adopted some inimical policies which created more disparities and tussles between the locals and refugees, cut employment opportunities, promoted discontent and a sense of alienation among the latter. It was a period of tremendous chaos for the refugees, but things did not end there. The Partition refugees, who encountered tough competition from the Punjabis and Pathans during the Ayub and Yahya regimes, had yet to face Bhutto's Sindhi nationalism. Several steps taken by the Bhutto Government to meet the long-standing demands of the Sindhis posed a threat to the Muhajirs' social, political and economic interests, and were indicative of Sindhi domination. The Muhajirs' resentment and isolation grew.

The clash and conflict between the Partition refugees and the local power-brokers became inevitable after the dismemberment of Pakistan in 1971. Every nationality and community began clamouring for its rights, and succeeding generations of Partition refugees had reason to be restless and disillusioned. However, the political activism of the refugees was often crushed with force. It was under these circumstances that the Muhajir Quami Movement (MQM) was born to fight for the rights of different generations of Partition refugees. It was later renamed the Muttahida Quami Movement or United National Movement. The creation of the MQM was a new factor in Pakistani politics, dominated by the feudal and tribal lords in league with the civil and military bureaucracy. Belonging to the middle classes, the MQM leaders had a decisive impact on the politics of Pakistan.

Apart from this, another significant aspect of migration was ethnic mobility, because the migration had a great effect on the ethnic politics of the country. Sind has always been a very important province in Pakistan. Before Independence, it was a relatively homogeneous province. The ethnic problems in Sind started with the arrival of the Partition refugees, and the spectre of ethnonationalism moved so quickly after the first decade of Pakistan's existence that the country has virtually remained hostage to the problem of ethnicity since its inception.

The large exodus of refugees not only led to a significant change in the demographic balance between the rural and urban sectors, but also strengthened the bureaucrats' hold over society. In Sind, a high proportion of refugees impacted on its political, economic and cultural life, as 27 per cent came from UP alone, and their ratios were more than 13 times higher in Sind than in Punjab. Many of the refugees were educated, skilled and filled with ambition to play their full role in the newly established country. They had connections with the higher-ups and the new State also extended to them comprehensive support. They therefore joined prime jobs in administration, got involved in business and actively supported the Pakistan Muslim League and its leaders. Their impact on Sind was therefore considerable.

The Partition refugees, specially the UP intelligentsia, had had a great mental distance from the other people of Sind in the sense that they had never experienced such domineering feudal patterns of politics as prevalent there. They came to Sind after Independence, and their greatest concentration was in Karachi and Hyderabad, but some, though in very small numbers, went to the towns in the interior as well.

The Partition refugees were absorbed in various departments and services of Pakistan, specially in the higher ranks of the civil bureaucracy. Their over-representation gave them an influential voice in policy making. Many others were employed in banks, businesses and new industries. The adoption of Urdu as Pakistan's official language and neglect of Sindhi, the specification of Karachi, Sind's largest city, as the 'federal capital area' and its subsequent removal from Sind provincial control, the award of properties and land left by the departing Sindhi Hindus to the refugees and Muhajirs, were all policies that further strengthened their hold and influenced dramatically the local culture. These developments led to the revitalization of Sindhi ethnicity because the Sindhis were victims of discrimination since Independence. They were poorly represented in the central bureaucracy in Sind itself. The police departments were generally manned by Punjabis, and all high posts of the government were occupied by non-Sindhis. The posts of chief secretary and Inspector-General of police were rarely, if ever, held by local Sindhis.

In this period of cataclysm, ethnic mobilization of Sindhis gained momentum. Sindhi alienation was aggravated by the Muhajir factor. The Sindhis felt hindrances in career advancement and other economic opportunities and employment: it naturally gave rise to conflict between the Sindhis and Muhajirs. Since the mid-1980s, Sind has suffered occasional bouts of ethnic violence. Moreover, riots in Hyderabad and Karachi between Partition refugees and the native Sindhi-speaking Sindhis have not only made the headlines of international media, but also posed as the main challenge to the fragile post-Zia regimes. Ethnic politics certainly took a bad turn in the mid-1980s, when the new generation of ethnic leaders—specially in urban Sind—took up arms.

Thereafter, the MQM resorted to coercive measures to suppress its opponents and indulged in urban guerrilla activities. Soon, a discreet campaign by the powerful in and out of government was started for 'ethnic cleansing' of the refugees. This led to acute ethnic tensions and a serious ethnic divide in Sind.

Several studies have been done on Pakistan's politics and economy and a few directly or indirectly deal with the issue of Karachi and the rise of the MQM as a new political phenomenon. However, a study on Partition refugees, their integration in Pakistani society, and the gradual alienation of the succeeding generations along with the ethnic situation has not been attempted so far. The need for such a study was always and is still there, because the impact of refugees on the movement against feudalism and tribalism may prove to be critical in the coming decades. The movement in favour of democracy and mobilization of civil society depends essentially on which side the Partition refugees align with—the authoritarian forces or the democratic forces in the Pakistan of tomorrow. A study covering these aspects of Pakistan's polity and the refugee's struggle for empowerment is clearly needed.

The present study is an attempt in this direction. It highlights Pakistan's positive approach towards the refugees, and explains the dynamics of social and cultural interaction in areas and regions where the native inhabitants and the new arrivals have learnt to live together. It also deals with the issues of terrorism, refugee tensions, marginalization of other groups, sectarianism, clash of interests, frequent outbreaks of violence in Karachi and urban Sind where the Partition refugees are concentrated. This work also looks at the simmering ethnic faultlines in Sind. It focuses on the post-1971 developments and speculates upon the prospects of local-refugee integration/alienation.

The study consists of six sections: an introduction, four chapters, and a conclusion. The Introduction discusses the contemporary migratory trends in the world in general and in Pakistan in particular. It also refers to the impact of the refugees on the receiving states including Pakistan and aspects of ethnicity. Chapter 1, 'Partition of India and Influx of Refugees' discusses the events leading to the Partition of India in 1947 and the subsequent violence, killing and uprooting of the people and Pakistan's response to the challenge. It focuses on the process of resettlement and reintegration. The problems, difficulties and challenges faced by Pakistan during the premiership of Liaquat Ali Khan, and the various initiatives and steps undertaken by his government to deal with the issue of distribution of evacuee property and award of citizenship are covered. Chapter 2, 'Pakistan and Partition Refugees in West Punjab, Kashmir and East Pakistan' discusses the complex issues of arrival of refugees, reception, resettlement and rehabilitation in other areas of Pakistan, viz., West Punjab, Kashmir, and East Pakistan. It also focuses on the sensitive issue of repatriation of stranded Pakistanis (Bihari refugees) and the role of the Pakistan Army. Chapter 3, 'Post-1958 Pakistan and Partition Refugees in Sind' deals with the political, economic, and social developments in Pakistan and their impact on Partition refugees. With the advent of the military regime of General Ayub Khan, the political, governmental and economic decline of the power and influence of Partition refugees commenced. It has continued since. This chapter covers these aspects and discusses the dubious and discriminating policies of Ayub Khan, Yahya Khan, Zulfiqar Ali Bhutto, and Zia-ul Haq towards Partition refugees and the circumstances which led to the formation of the MQM. Chapter 4, 'Partition Refugees: Struggle for Empowerment and State's Response' discusses the causes of refugee uprisings in Karachi/ Pakistan, the gradual empowerment of the refugees, and strategies and actions of the Pakistani establishment to contain and control this emerging political force. It also covers the MQM's political role, strategies and tactics and various alliances between the MQM and the establishment and their functions. It also refers to the violence, killing and ethnicization of Karachi, and highlights the movement of the MQM against the military, the bureaucracy and intelligence agencies.

The present study maintains that the Partition refugees can play the role of catalyst in the movement against feudalism, tribalism, militarism and political violence if they are allowed sufficient political and intellectual leverage, and if the MQM develops into a credible, democratic and progressive force.

A number of questions have been raised in this study. These, briefly, include the following:

1. Why were Indian Muslims uprooted and forced to come to Pakistan?
2. What was the response of the newly-born state of Pakistan?
3. Why did local-refugee tensions develop, and what was the role of the state in inflaming/reducing the tension?
4. What were the responses of the Partition refugees to the strategies to disempower them?
5. To what extent have the Partition refugees attained empowerment?
6. What is the future of Partition refugees?

The present study has been conducted with the following objectives in mind:

1. To conduct an in-depth study in order to appreciate the problems faced by the Partition refugees and the response of the newly-created state of Pakistan to provide security and dignity to them and help them integrate in Pakistan.
2. To study the causes of the disenchantment of both the local population and the Partition refugees and the magnitude of the problem.
3. To examine the strategies and moves of the state to disempower the Partition refugees.

4. To study the dynamics of the movement of Partition refugees for empowerment and for acceptance by the local people as equal partners.
5. To speculate upon the future of Partition refugees and the future of Pakistan.

I have consulted a number of primary and secondary sources while studying the issues involved. However, I was largely handicapped because of unavailability of basic data and a dearth of primary source material. While interviews with prominent citizens of Pakistan were conducted, many have asked that their names not that be mentioned while referring to their comments being quoted in the study: their remarks have had to be used off the record. Major published material was equally scanty. I consulted whatever was available. As far as the methodology is concerned, historical, analytical, and scientific approaches have been followed and the published materials have been carefully analysed. It is really unfortunate that a lot of important information, provided by some distinguished Pakistanis could not be quoted or included in this study.

CHAPTER 1

Partition of India and Influx of Refugees

The Partition of British India took place on the night of 14/15 August 1947 and two independent states, India and Pakistan, came into being. The States were created in the midst of violence, hatred and calls for revenge. Further, the partition of both Bengal and Punjab caused large-scale uprooting of Muslims, Hindus and Sikhs. Indeed, the great divide of 1947 is a sad story, as it resulted in the unprecedented bloodshed of about 100,000 people while migrating to their cherished land to breathe the air of freedom. The founder of the state of Pakistan, Quaid-i-Azam Mohammed Ali Jinnah, was greatly distressed at such colossal loss of life and property.[1]

It was widely feared that the mounting Hindu-Muslim and Muslim-Sikh tensions would take a toll, but not many expected such a large-scale communal bloodshed on the eve of Partition and thereafter. It is true that the 1946 massacre of Muslims in Bihar was the first organized killing of opponents over a wide area, but the orgy of destruction had no long-term end in view and was quickly terminated. In contrast, the Sikhs had planned the Punjab massacres on a much larger scale. They desired the attainment of various political objectives through uncontrolled violence and terror. The Sikhs started a military campaign that was to end only when their objectives were attained. They had at their disposal trained armed forces from Hindu and Sikh princely states and had planned to start the massacres at a time when the administration in East and West Punjab would be stretched to the

[1] M. Shafique Ahmed, 'The Birth of Quaid-i-Azam', *Daily Dawn* (Karachi), 25 December 2002.

limit quelling the widespread violence. The Hindu and Sikh rulers played a despicable part in this horrible tragedy.[2]

In 1947, the communal disturbances overshadowed everything else in India. Some 500,000 people were massacred and some 12 million citizens had to leave their homes.[3] Punjab was the worst-affected area. The riots were so frequent there that it was difficult to keep track of them all.[4] The condition in East Punjab was worse than in West Punjab, because the Sikhs were better armed and better organized. In Amritsar and in its vicinity, the Sikhs had formed armed bands, which carried out raids on the Muslim-majority villages. They were well-organized and often included mounted men.[5]

The refugees from East Punjab in 1947 were the worst sufferers of the 'ethnic cleansing' of 1947. These Muslims had lost homes, possessions, and in many cases members of their immediate families. Almost every migrant family from the Indian Punjab was a sad spectacle, as many of them had to flee from their ancestral lands, unprepared for the hardships ahead.[6] The *Times* special correspondent in the Punjab reported that 'The Sikhs are clearing Eastern Punjab of the Muslims, butchering hundreds daily, forcing thousands to flee westward, burning Muslim villages and homesteads.' In his view, the violence was organized from the highest level of the Sikh leadership and it was done systematically, sector by sector. According to the report, former soldiers often led the Sikh bands or *jathas*.[7]

Likewise, in the North-West Frontier Province (NWFP), rioting,

[2] Chaudhri Mohammad Ali, *The Emergence of Pakistan*, Lahore: Research Society of Pakistan, University of Punjab, 1973, p. 254.

[3] Massarrat Sohail, *Partition and Anglo-Pakistan Relations: 1947–51*, Karachi, Lahore, Islamabad: Vanguard Books, 1991, p. 88.

[4] Ibid. See Governor of Punjab's Report to the Viceroy, 13 August 1947, TP, XII, 459.

[5] Ibid. Note by Auchinleck, 15 August 1947, TP, XII, 486.

[6] Iftikhar H. Malik, *State and Civil Society in Pakistan: Politics of Authority, Ideology and Ethnicity*, New York, London: St. Martins Press, Macmillan Press, 1997 p. 199.

[7] Sohail, op. cit., n. 3 above, p. 88.

looting and arson were reported from Dera Ismail Khan. Half the city went up in flames, there were incidents in Calcutta (now Kolkata), and a curfew was imposed at night in Bombay (now Mumbai). Many other cities including Benaras (now Varanasi) went up in flames.[8]

The press and unofficial reports from Delhi indicated that murder, arson, and looting continued in broad daylight, and the government often seemed powerless in dealing with the armed mobs, mainly led by the Sikhs.[9]

Many incidents of attacks on passengers waiting for trains at Delhi Railway Station were reported.[10] The Hindus were in close alliance with the Sikhs, and Hindu fundamentalist organizations such as the Rashtriya Swayamsevak Sangh (RSS) cooperated with them in acts of organized violence.[11] Some of the instigators of disturbance arrested by the Punjab police gave statements which implicated Master Tara Singh, one of the most prominent leaders of the Akali Dal, obtained assistance, encouraged manufacture of bombs and the collection of arms through Sikh army officers. He was also reported to be involved in plans to blow up Pakistan-special trains carrying Muslims from Delhi to Lahore and Karachi. A Sikh plan to assassinate Jinnah during the Independence Day ceremonies at Karachi on 15 August was also discovered.[12] On 2 March, Master Tara Singh most dramatically unsheathed his sword and shouted, 'The time has come when the might of the sword alone shall rule. The Sikhs are ready, we have to bring the Muslims to their senses.' The Hindu leaders expressed more or less the

[8] H.V. Hodson, *The Great Divide: Britain-India-Pakistan*, Karachi: Oxford University Press, 1969, p. 266.

[9] Sohail, op. cit., n. 3 above, p. 89; also see 'Disturbances in the Punjab', R 3/1/173, IQR, 13 Sept. 1947.

[10] Ibid., p. 90. For details, see document Tel, UKHC (1) to CRO, 9 Sept. 1947.

[11] Ali, op. cit., n. 2 above, p. 193.

[12] Sohail, op. cit., n. 3 above, p. 71. This statement is by Captain Savage, a police officer in the Punjab CID 'Control', who was employed in investigation of disturbance cases: 'Record of mtg. between Viceroy, Jinnah and Patel', 5 August 1947, TP, XII, 345.

same sentiments. The threat did not end there.[13] On 4 March, in spite of the official ban on processions, Bhim Sen Sachar, a minister in the Punjab, resigned and led a big Hindu-Sikh procession to the Assembly chamber in Lahore. Near the chamber, Sachar told the procession and other non-Muslims gathered there: 'I, as a member of the government, hereby declare that you have every right to take out processions.' Tara Singh shouted before the crowd, *Pakistan Murdabad* (Death to Pakistan) and *Raj karega Khalsa, baki rahe na koi* (The Sikh will rule, none else will remain).[14]

Communal riots started immediately in Lahore, and spread to Amritsar, Rawalpindi and Multan within the next 48 hours. On 15 August, the day of liberation was celebrated strangely in the Punjab. During the afternoon, a Sikh mob paraded a number of Muslim women naked through the streets of Amritsar, raped them and then hacked some of them to pieces with *kirpans* and burnt the others alive.[15] The Sikhs marched out in well-disciplined, well-guarded convoys, nourishing a fierce hate for those who had compelled them to abandon their carefully nurtured fields. They found their compatriots in India in a bloodthirsty mood. As trains heading to Pakistan carrying Muslim clerks and artisans neared Amritsar (the last station before the Pakistan border), the Sikh fanatics, fell upon them with their cruel swords. Trainloads of the dead and dying crossed into Pakistan, and fear spread fast.[16]

On 8 August, a train was derailed after it had left Bathinda Junction in East Punjab. The railway line was blown up by a guncotton slab detonated electrically. Three railway bogeys were smashed and three derailed. A number of bombs connected by wire were placed on the tracks to blow up the train completely, but luckily, only one bomb exploded and the casualties were slight.[17]

[13] Chaudhri Khaliquzzaman, *Pathway to Pakistan*, Lahore: Longmans Green, 1961, p. 376.

[14] Latif Ahmed Sherwani, *The Partition of India, and Mountbatten*, Karachi: Council for Pakistan Studies, 1986, pp. 101–2.

[15] Ali, op. cit., n. 2 above, p. 256; John Connell, *Auchinleck*, London: Cassell, 1959, p. 906.

[16] Hugh Tinker, *India and Pakistan: A Political Analysis*, London: Pall Mall Press, 2nd edn., 1967, pp. 35–6.

[17] Ali, op. cit., n. 2 above, p. 199.

Muslims were also participating in violence and had launched reprisals against the Hindus and Sikhs who were still living in West Punjab and against those who were migrating to India. The worst violence took place in Sheikhupura in August 1947, where killing, stabbing, burning and rioting continued for twenty-four hours at a stretch. One report says that a large number of Hindu and Sikh women committed suicide to save themselves from brutal attacks by the Muslims. In addition attack and stabbing of passengers in trains also started and attacks by Muslims on refugee trains were reported from Wazirabad, Narwal and Raiwand, and the railway stations became a scene of wholesale carnage. In other incidents, many non-Muslims were stabbed in Mugalpura Railway Workshop and killings also took place in other districts. The tragedies of Partition would not have been complete had they not been accompanied, as every conflict since the dawn of history, by an outpouring of sexual savagery. Nearly all the atrocities cursing the province were embellished by orgies of rape. Tens of thousands of girls and women were seized from refugee columns, crowded trains, isolated villages, in the most widespread orgy of modern times. The Sikhs' tenth Guru had specifically enjoined his followers against sexual intercourse with Muslim women to prevent what had happened in the Punjab. The inevitable result was a legend among the Sikhs that Muslim women were capable of particular prowess.[18] Under the impact of events in Punjab, the Sikhs forgot their Guru's admonishment and gave free rein to their fantasies. With morbid frenzy, they fell on Muslims everywhere. Kidnapped Muslim girls were herded in large number in their parts of Punjab.[19] The *Times* special correspondent in Punjab reported on 23 August that the Sikh *jathas* in particular were carrying out 'appalling atrocities', including the cold-blooded mass murder of men, women, and children in a number of villages, often accompanied by mutilation, that the Sikhs were 'cleansing the East Punjab of Moslems'. Some large towns like Amritsar and Jullundur (now

[18] Larry Collins and Dominique Lapierre, *Freedom at Midnight*, New Delhi: Vikas Publishing, 1975–6, pp. 336–7.

[19] Ibid., p. 337.

Jalandhar) were now quieter because there were no Muslims left.[20]

Shocked and dismayed, Jinnah expressed his deep distress and emphasized in a radio broadcast from Lahore on 31 August 1947 that Pakistan was achieved without bloodshed. He added: 'Are we now going to besmear the great achievement for which there is no parallel in the history of the world by resorting to frenzy, savagery and butchery?'[21]

The Pakistan Government soon got busy in looking after the refugees and working towards their rehabilitation. The early years from 1947 to 1951 were marked by a struggle for national survival. The task, by any criterion, was challenging. The exigencies of creating a state and dealing with a number of problems relating to governance, finance, the law and order situation, communication, transport, water supply, trade and economy were demanding.

Further, the refusal of India to hand over the assets amounting to over 1,000 crores (10 lakh equals 1 million, and 10 million equals 1 crore) due to Pakistan under the Partition Agreement created unprecedented problems. Circumstances such as these required prompt measures. Jinnah devoted all his energies to nation-building and dealing with the challenges with great insight, firmness and resolution. After his death in September 1948, Liaquat Ali Khan, as Prime Minister, continued his mission. He guided the government, the Muslim League, and the Constituent Assembly. The defence forces were organized and various disputes with India with regard to the refugees and minorities were settled, law and order was maintained, and trade and commerce enhanced. His ceaseless efforts showed his involvement in the country, nation and matters of refugees. Delivering a speech at the Town Hall, Washington, DC on 8 May 1950, he said:

> We began from scratch, in our offices there were few chairs and tables and few typewriters. As soon as we hoisted our new flag in our new capital, Karachi, two-way mass-migration between India and Pakistan started accompanied by great sufferings and heart-rending misery. Within

[20] Saleem Ullah Khan, *The Journey to Pakistan: Documentation on Refugees of 1947*, Islamabad: National Documentation Centre, 1993, p. 318.

[21] Ibid., p. 320.

a few months seven million people crossed over from India into our country to seek shelter. Most of them were poor farmers who, when they came over, had no work, no land, no tools, no cattle. They were frightened and dazed. Some had not eaten for many days. Many families had lost parents, children, on the way, with little hope of recovering them. For a moment we asked ourselves, shall we, a new underdeveloped and ill-equipped country, be able to stand this shock? It was a tremendous test of our belief in ourselves. Even our friends were skeptical and shook their heads. We ourselves, I frankly confess, were a little nervous but our national cohesion and the fortitude and the spirit of self-sacrifice of the common man and the common woman surpassed everyone's expectations.[22]

Pakistan came into existence on 14 August 1947 without possessing the basic requirements of a State: its geographical frontiers were yet to be determined; it was without a seat of government or an administrative structure; its Armed Forces were scattered; its civil servants, police officers and soldiers were in the midst of migrating from India. The economic and political systems were completely disturbed, and the communication system had broken down.

The administrative and economic machinery was yet to be rescued from its Indian connection and established as a new body to conform to the new boundaries drawn by the British Government and Pakistan had to deal with the millions of refugees streaming in. Again, Pakistan had no resources apart from agricultural land. It had few banks and no head office of any major firm. There were no commercial, financial and industrial centres like those in Calcutta and Bombay in India. The major provinces of India (apart from Bengal and the Punjab) had their territory intact and their government machinery untouched by the consequences of Partition. The public servants continued to work and most of the communication system remained intact. The Indian Government was clearly well-equipped to handle the problems of Partition.

[22] Extracts from the speech of Shaheed-e-Millat Liaquat Ali Khan delivered in the Town Hall, Washington, DC, 8 May 1950, referred to in Ziauddin Ahmed *Liaquat Ali Khan: Builder of Pakistan*, Karachi: Royal Books, 1990, p. 216.

In Pakistan, the areas producing raw materials such as jute, cotton, hides and skin were deprived of the processing units. The new boundary of the Punjab had cut across the irrigation system leaving vital headworks in Kashmir and India. Likewise, the eastern wing lost the principal port of Calcutta, railway junctions and the whole industrial complex. In the exodus that followed Partition, West Pakistan was deprived of merchants, bankers, traders, teachers, doctors and technical professionals, who were almost entirely non-Muslims.

On the other hand, the seven million refugees from India needed immediate rehabilitation. Pakistan was in a desperate situation. Partition had left bitterness. The Hindu leaders regarded Pakistan as a transient euphoria of the Muslims. Its collapse was considered imminent. Millions of refugees had arrived with harrowing stories. Freedom for Pakistan had got off to a bad start. India refused delivery of military equipment, division of assets, disposition of evacuees property, and the distribution of canal water. The princely state of Kashmir became a constant source of friction between the two countries. Worse, India stopped the supply of irrigation water to canals running through Pakistani Punjab. Within ten weeks of Independence, the two states were locked in violent confrontation.[23] During these weeks and months of great challenges and insecurities, Pakistan, under the leadership of Jinnah, grappled with the issues confidently, with Jinnah stressing public order as the need of the hour. In his first address to the Constituent Assembly on 11 August 1947, he had underlined the urgency of law and order to protect the life, property, and religious beliefs of the subjects. Subsequently, he stressed, again and again, on the need to protect the life and honour of the refugees and to care for and assist them.

Small-scale migration from one part of the country to another had began a little before Independence, but as a result of widespread rioting and looting of property in the wake of Independence, it assumed massive proportions immediately after freedom was attained. Millions crossed the newly-created borders, many of them

[23] Zarina Salamat, *Pakistan 1947–58: A Historical Review*, Islamabad: National Institute of Historical and Cultural Research, 1992, p. 27.

with nothing except the clothes they wore and the horrifying memories of their near and dear ones killed before their eyes and their women abducted. This tragedy affected the lives of the people uprooted from places where they had lived for generations. For a long time, they found it difficult to adjust themselves to a different social and economic milieu. Before the joint organization of the exodus by the Indian and Pakistani Governments, the refugee columns were in constant fear of attack by armed marauders, many refugees losing their lives in attacks along the route, others being robbed, and a number of women and girls being abducted.[24]

As to how difficult the task of caring and providing for the refugees was can be gauged from the following passage on refugee arrival and rehabilitation:

> Columns of the refugees were spread out over miles of roads and fields. During the day, pale clouds of dust churned by the hooves of thousands of buffaloes and bullocks hung above each column, stains along the horizon plotted the refugees' advance. At night, collapsing by the side of the road, the refugees burnt thousands of little fires to cook their few scraps of food. From a distance, the light of their fires diffused by the dust settling above the columns merged into one dull red glow. Lying on the ground, insecure, hungry and exhausted, the numb and wretched creatures could realize the awfulness of what was happening to them with their eyes and throats raw with dust, feet bruised by stones or the searing asphalt, tortured by hunger and thirst, enrobed in a stench of urine, sweat and defecation, the refugees plodded dumbly forward. They flowed on in filthy *dhotis*, *saris*, trousers, frayed sandals, sometimes only one shoe, often none at all; elderly women clung to their sons, pregnant women to their husbands. Men carried invalid wives and mothers on their shoulder, women their infants. They had to endure their burden not for a mile or two but for a hundred, two hundred miles, for days on end with nothing to nourish their strength but a chapatti (a flat unleavened bread) and a few sips of water.[25]

The main problem for the receiving state was to secure as early and orderly an evacuation and settlement of the refugees as possible.

[24] Keesing's Research Report 9, *Pakistan from 1947 to the Creation of Bangladesh*, New York: Charles Scribner's Sons, 1971, p. 12.

[25] Collins and Lapierre, op. cit., n. 18 above, p. 320.

The greatest mass migration in history was under way: within weeks, 12 million people had left their homes and gone forth on foot, by bullock cart, by railway, by car and by plane to seek shelter and safety in the other dominion. In its issue of 4 September 1947, the *Times* reported 20-mile-long columns of refugees and estimated the number at twenty thousand. Most of them were on foot and moving towards Pakistan. They had no earthly possessions; they had tasted misery, seen babies killed, corpses mutilated, and women dishonoured. Death had stalked them on the way. Tens of thousands had died on the road because of starvation and disease, or been killed by the armed Sikh gangs.

The task of feeding, clothing, settling and rehabilitating these millions of Partition refugees was quite daunting. When they entered Lahore and other places in Pakistani Punjab, the local inhabitants went forth to share food and clothing with them and assisted them. The locals came forward voluntarily and readily underwent hardships for the sake of rehabilitating the refugees. It is true that there were selfish and hard-hearted residents who took advantage of the prevailing conditions and fraudulently took possession of the evacuees properties in Pakistan.[26]

In the beginning of September 1947, the Ministry of Refugees and Rehabilitation was formed in Pakistan and the Emergency Committee of the Cabinet was set up. But long before that, and even before 15 August, the movement of Muslim refugees from Amritsar district to Pakistan had started as a result of communal disturbances.[27] On 11 September, the West Punjab Government appointed a rehabilitation commissioner for the province.[28] By the middle of October, a Pakistan Punjab Council was set up. One of the first initiatives of this organization was a joint military evacuation scheme in cooperation with the Military Evacuation Organisations (MEO) of both governments.[29] Simultaneously, the need was felt for a joint organization of the Central Government

[26] Ali, op. cit., n. 2 above, pp. 261–2.

[27] Khan, op. cit., n. 20 above, p. 58.

[28] Ibid., p. 323.

[29] Ibid., p. 59.

and the Government of West Punjab, the province most concerned with the problem of Partition refugees. Accordingly, the Punjab Refugees Council for Pakistan was formed. To be presided over by the prime minister, its members included the governor and chief minister of West Punjab and central and provincial refugee ministers. Later, similar joint refugee councils were set up in the NWFP and in Sind. The MEO was established with its headquarters at Lahore, and the Indian MEO originally had its headquarters at Amritsar.[30]

As a matter of fact, when Partition was being agreed upon, it was expected that the old conflicts would gradually be buried and that the minority communities living in the two states would be assured an honourable existence on the basis of full equality. As such, both Indian and Pakistani ministers treated the communal problem as a high-priority issue and endeavoured to protect and save the rights of the minorities on both sides of the frontiers. Both Jinnah and Gandhi enthusiastically supported their efforts and the ruling parties of the two states solemnly pledged to a policy of non-discrimination against any section of their citizens. The Congress leaders had repeatedly promised that they would safeguard the rights of the Indian Muslims and other minorities.[31] The Muslim League in Pakistan pledged full protection and respect for the rights of Hindus and other minorities. Both for the Muslims in India and for the Hindus in East Pakistan, it was not a question of legitimate political rights, but one of being just allowed to lead a peaceful life. For the minorities, even when the nightmare of the 1947 riots was still fresh in their minds with several millions of them having migrated in either direction to start a new life in new surroundings, and with a million dead and injured in the holocaust, a fresh wave of trouble developed in East Pakistan.

It may be stated here that unlike in West and East Punjab, things were generally normal in Bengal except for what had happened in Calcutta on the eve of Independence Day and the

[30] Ali, op. cit., n. 2 above, p. 263.

[31] Mazhar Ali Khan, *Pakistan: The First Twelve Years*, Karachi: Oxford University Press, 1996, p. 67.

day after.[32] For Indian Muslims; the position was getting increasingly difficult. It was repeatedly stressed at public platforms, in the press and in the Parliament that the support for the demand for Pakistan came mainly from the Muslims in the states where they were in a minority.[33] Avenues for employment were severely restricted for the Indian Muslims and discriminatory laws were used to deprive many of their property and their loyalty to the state was suspect.[34] With the arrival of the Muslims from India, tension mounted in Karachi, interior Sind, and in the Punjab and rendered the remaining Hindu and Sikh minorities very vulnerable. The Islamic rhetoric of political leaders in Pakistan further distanced the Hindus from the emerging state. Soon enough, the situation deteriorated in East Pakistan. In November 1949, stories of the confiscation of Hindu property in East Bengal featured prominently in the Indian press. Also reported were tales of gruesome molestation and harassment of Hindus there. On 25 November, the West Bengal Government's protest to the East Bengal Government was published, and on 14 December, the Government of India protested formally to the Pakistan Government. There were some other factors forcing a showdown. The influx of refugees from East Bengal encouraged a group in West Bengal to press for their settlement in the districts bordering East Pakistan. On 20 January 1950, the Calcutta Press published an account of police atrocities on the Hindu population of Khulna in East Bengal.[35] Around 18 January, serious communal disturbances broke out in Dacca (now Dhaka), and on 13 February, riots took place at Feni, a subdivision of Noakhali district, and in the town of Barisal in East Bengal. Between 16 and 20 February, trouble spread in the rural areas of East Bengal.

When news of this rioting filtered back into West Bengal, the smouldering communal violence in Calcutta erupted into sporadic

[32] Mohammad Reza Khan, *What Price Freedom?*, Karachi: Kutub Printers, 1977, p. 427.

[33] Ibid., p. 428.

[34] Ali Khan, op. cit., n. 31 above, p. 68.

[35] Reza Khan, op. cit., n. 32 above, p. 430.

mob action and individual reprisals. In extremist circles in India, this appeared as a well-laid plot to kill off or drive out the Hindus from East Bengal; on the Pakistani side, it assumed the character of a 'master plan' of Sardar Patel, Deputy Prime Minister of India,[36] to push the remaining Indian Muslims to Pakistan. However, the crisis was averted when an agreement was reached on 8 April 1950 at New Delhi to ensure to the minorities, throughout their territories, complete equality of citizenship irrespective of religion. The part of the agreement which applied to the general relations between the two countries reiterated a principle enunciated earlier in the Calcutta agreement of April 1948. It stated that the allegiance and loyalty of the minorities was to the state of which they were citizens, and it was to the government of their own state that they must look to redress their grievances.[37]

The Nehru–Liaquat Pact of 1950 was an important document and contributed substantially to the easing of tensions between the two states. In addition, it drove the states towards working more seriously for the resettlement of the refugees and for finding durable solutions concerning the refugees. When the communal riots and Partition took place in 1947, the refugees from East Punjab decided to move to West Punjab, whereas many emigrants from UP, central India, and the former state of Hyderabad decided to move to Sind. The Muslims of Delhi generally opted for West Punjab.[38] The abrupt and violent nature of migration from Indian Punjab to Pakistan left these refugees in a disadvantaged position.[39] The total number of Indian Muslims was around one hundred million, out of which 65 million became Pakistani nationals and the remaining 35–40 million remained in India. At the time of Independence, Muslims in the province of undivided Bengal and Punjab accounted for 55–8 per cent of the total population.[40] West Punjab had received 59.26 lakh people against only 38.08 lakh. West Punjab rehabilitated 21.18 lakh people in excess of

[36] Ibid., p. 431.
[37] Ibid., p. 432.
[38] Malik, op. cit., n. 6 above, p. 200.
[39] Ibid., p. 199.
[40] Ibid.

those that it lost. The migration increased the population of West Punjab (Pakistan) from 172.46 lakh to 193.64 lakh, and reduced the population of East Punjab (India) and the state from 189.68 lakh to 168.50 lakh.[41] Sind received more refugees than it had sent and welcomed them enthusiastically.

Thus, urban areas in the two provinces became centres of refugee concentration. Lahore and Karachi became huge population centres overnight.[42] The local population, entertaining high hopes of a peaceful coexistence with their Muslim brothers, welcomed the influx of 'Hindustanis' (Indian refugees) in both wings, and agreed to share the citizenship of a newly-Independent state. Soon after Independence, the dispute over Kashmir, Junagarh and Hyderabad led a new wave of emigrants to Pakistan. India happily got rid of 'extra' Muslims from its soil. Independence had led to the emigration of Hindus and Sikhs from Pakistani provinces, which had received 2 million more refugees than India in the exchange.

According to the Census of 1951, 49 per cent of the total population in Karachi was refugee; in Hyderabad, 71 per cent; and in Lahore, the refugee population was 43 per cent of the total population.[43] The urban population compared to that of rural Sind in the post-1951 years had increased noticeably, with the Muhajirs forming a visible majority in cities like Karachi and Hyderabad.[44] The refugees from UP and elsewhere in northern India continued to migrate till 1951.[45] The vacuum left by urban and commercial Hindus was filled not by the Muslim Sindhis, but by well-educated, mobile Muhajirs whose mother tongue became the national language and who began establishing their own businesses, industries and financial concerns in Karachi, Hyderabad and Sukkur.[46] These Urdu-speaking refugees preferred Karachi

[41] Khan, op. cit., n. 20 above, pp. 16–17.

[42] Malik, op. cit., n. 6 above, p. 200.

[43] A. Tayyab, *Pakistan: A Political Geography*, Karachi: Oxford University Press, 1966, pp. 171–2; ibid., p. 200.

[44] Ibid., p. 202.

[45] Ibid., p. 199.

[46] Ibid.

because it was the centre of industry. Further, it was also the city of the Quaid and Liaquat Ali Khan.

The provincial Government of Sind made great efforts to assist the refugees. The Quaid-i-Azam made an appeal on 12 September 1947 for a fund to be known as the 'Quaid-i-Azam's Relief Fund'. He said, 'Let every man and woman resolve from this day to live henceforth strictly on an austerity basis in respect of foodstuff, clothing, . . . thus saved be brought to this common pool for the relief of the stricken. The winter is approaching and in the Punjab and Delhi particularly, it is severe and we must provide refugees protection against it.' A central committee of six members administrated the Quaid-i-Azam's Relief Fund. The committee consisted of the Quaid-i-Azam, the finance minister, minister of refugees, evacuees and rehabilitation, the governor of Sind, the president of the Sind Provincial Muslim League and the auditor-general of Pakistan. For the improvement of the work, provincial committees were set up. The Quaid appealed to the nation to contribute to the Quaid-i-Azam's Relief Fund and said:

> I appeal to the nation to come forward with generous contribution to this fund and to stint no sacrifices or efforts for this purpose. There are millions who are living in safety and security and enjoying the comforts of life while countless numbers of their fellow human beings have suffered and are suffering grievously. Now is the time for the former to make the greatest possible voluntary sacrifices of comfort and of the material things. The government and myself have been spending the best part of our time and energy in dealing with this grave crisis, which continues to assume greater proportions as one disaster follows another. We have now to think in terms of affording relief to those millions of our brethren who have been stricken by this calamity. The nation is aware that an Emergency Committee of the cabinet has been constituted for the purpose of rehabilitation. We are determined to mobilize resources of the state to the fullest extent to cope with this colossal task and to overcome all difficulties. ... In these circumstances, I have every hope and feel confident that our people will rise to the occasion and give all support to me that is possible for them to give.[47]

[47] Khan, op. cit., n. 20 above, pp. 255–7.

On 17 September 1947, he, accompanied by his sister, Fatima Jinnah, paid a surprise visit to the refugees' centre in Karachi.[48]

Despite the Liaquat–Nehru Pact of 1951, trans-border migration continued unabated. An important issue receiving great attention by the pact was the issue of evacuee property. Owing to the migration of non-Muslims from Pakistan to India and of Muslims from India to Pakistan on a mass scale, the problem of evacuee property had developed into a very complex problem for India and Pakistan. According to the Indian Ministry of Rehabilitation, about 9,000,000 Hindus and Sikhs had migrated to India from Pakistan and some 7,900,000 Muslims had moved from India to Pakistan. But according to the Pakistan Government, by 1950, no less than 8,000,000 Muslims had migrated from India, and 5,500,000 Hindus and Sikhs[49] had left the territories of West Pakistan. These migrants left most of their moveable and immovable properties in their native places.

The evacuee property problem called into existence a new body of legislation and government orders providing a fine harvest for lawyers and additional worry for private citizens. The orbit of these laws was widened gradually, so that the members of communities having nothing to do with the Hindu-Muslim controversy were directly affected and threatened by them.[50]

The property, both moveable and immovable, left behind by the refugees on both sides of the frontier was of considerable volume. According to an Indian source, the non-Muslim refugees vacated 6,729,000 acres of land in West Punjab (West Pakistan) alone, of which 4,307,000 were canal-irrigated; other lands relinquished by the non-Muslims were in Sind, NWFP, Bahawalpur, Baluchistan, and Khairpur.[51] According to calculations made in India, the tentative figures for the non-Muslims' evacuee properties

[48] Ibid., p. 258.

[49] Mohammad Ahsen Chaudhri, 'Evacuee Property in India and Pakistan', *Pakistan Horizon*, vol. 10, no. 2, April–June 1957, p. 96; Government of Pakistan, *The Evacuee Property Problem: Pakistan's Case*, Karachi: Government of Pakistan, 1950, p. 3.

[50] Ibid., p. 97.

in West Pakistan were as follows: urban houses: 500,000 (approx.); building plots: 22,000; industrial properties: 12,000.

Agricultural land abandoned in West Pakistan amounted to approximately 9,000,000 acres, the major portion of which was rich canal-irrigated land; over one million rural houses, adjacent to agricultural lands as well as independent, were also abandoned. In addition, there were over 7,000 properties belonging to religious, charitable, educational and other trusts and endowments. The Government of India claimed that the figures were obtained after verification of the claims registered by the refugees under the Displaced Persons (Claims) Act, 1950.[52]

The Muslim refugees from East Punjab and the states of Patiala, Nabha, Jind, Faridkot, and Kapurthala in India abandoned 4,735,000 acres of land, 1,326,000 of which was irrigated.[53] In addition, houses, factories, machinery and huge stores of raw materials were left behind in India. Indian sources estimate the total value of Hindu and Sikh properties in Pakistan at $8 billion, and that of Muslim refugees' property in India at $800 million.[54] Evacuee properties left by the Muslims in India were calculated as follows: urban buildings: 287,000; building plots: 10,000; industrial undertakings: 1,700; agricultural land: approximately 5,800,000 acres of comparatively much inferior quality.[55]

These figures and other figures given by independent sources were contested by the two governments, but there was an inclination to sort out the issue.

In fact, the issue of evacuee property was first discussed on 29 August 1947 at a meeting of the Joint Defence Council of India and Pakistan. It was attended by the prime ministers of both

[51] Government of India, Ministry of Rehabilitation, November 1952 (latest figures).

[52] Jyoti Bhushan Das Gupta, *Indo-Pakistan Relations 1947–1955*, Amsterdam: Djam Batan, 1958, pp. 188–89.

[53] Government of India, op. cit., n. 51 above.

[54] *Concerning Evacuee Property*, issued by Ministry of Information and Broadcasting, Government of India, Delhi, 1950, p. 6.

[55] Jyoti, op. cit., n. 52 above, p. 189; 'Frozen Fortunes', India information service, New Delhi, March 1953, p. 3.

the countries under the chairmanship of Lord Mountbatten, Governor-General of India. An official communiqué issued on 30 August 1947 stated[56] that each government would appoint a custodian of refugee property, and close liaison between the custodians would be arranged. Moreover, the representatives of India and Pakistan reaffirmed that illegal seizure of property would not be recognized.[57] Five days later, on 3 September, the prime ministers of India and Pakistan issued a statement to the people of East and West Punjab which repeated that illegal seizure of property would not be recognized.[58] The central idea behind the joint action was to restore the properties to their rightful owners and to ensure the return of migrants from the places of refuge to their home countries and to appoint a custodian in each country to protect such properties against misappropriation. Both governments implemented the declaration through suitable executive enactments. The West Punjab Government, by an ordinance issued on 9 September 1947, provided for the appointment of a custodian who was to take charge of the evacuee property within his area with a view to preserving the same,[59] pending restoration to their rightful owners on payment of the dues to the same custodian (Sections 3 and 9).[60] The word 'evacuee' was defined as a person 'resident' in West Punjab (Pakistan) who left West Punjab on or after the first day of March 1947, without designating any person to look after his property in his absence. A similar ordinance was issued by the Government of East Punjab (India) on 14 September 1947. This ordinance was later extended to cover the Delhi province and Ajmer–Marwara. Both the ordinances recognized the rights of the owners to own the property abandoned by them.[61]

The concern for evacuee property was clearly a noble cause.

[56] Jyoti, op. cit., n. 52 above, p. 190.

[57] Ibid., p. 190; *India News*, London, 4 September 1947.

[58] *Concerning Evacuee Property*, op. cit., n. 54 above, p. 9.

[59] Jyoti, op. cit., n. 52 above, pp. 190–91; 'West Punjab Evacuee Property (Preservation) Ordinance, 1947', *The West Punjab Gazette*, Extraordinary Issue, Lahore, 10 September 1947.

[60] Ibid., p. 191.

[61] Chaudhri, op. cit., n. 49 above, pp. 97–8.

However, both Pakistan and India played politics with the idea and tried to embarrass each other. There was a lot of mistrust and it slowed down the implementation of decisions. This was especially more difficult in the case of urban immovable properties in Karachi, Delhi, Lahore, Calcutta and other places. Differences between the two states arose soon after the signing of the Karachi Agreement in 1949.

On 1 April 1949, for instance, the Government of India demanded revision of the Karachi Agreement, which had been signed only three months earlier. India proceeded to insist on a provision for the settlement of the question of urban property on a 'government to government' basis. Pakistan declined to agree to a revision of the Karachi Agreement, mainly on the ground that the agreement was not fairly tried out. On 7 April 1949, Pakistan's Minister of Rehabilitation, in a letter to the Government of India wrote:

> I should like to say that in my opinion it is too soon after our last agreement to make any major changes. We should give the agreement a fair trial; but if there are any difficulties, not involving major changes in policy, these I suggest, could be approximately discussed in our inter-dominion commission meeting.[62]

India, however, proceeded to extend its evacuee property law to places other than the agreed areas. The Karachi Agreement had intended that the operation of these laws be restricted to those areas from which there were movements of minority peoples. Pakistan protested against the extended application of the laws to the whole of India (except West Bengal, Assam, Cooch Behar, Tripura and Manipur), but India rejected the protest.[63] Thus, in a few months, the Karachi Agreement became an object of dispute.[64]

Refugees from East Punjab who had migrated to West Punjab in 1947 didn't have time to collect their personal valuables,

[62] Ibid., pp. 100–1; quoted in *Evacuee Property Dispute*, published by the Govt. of Pakistan Ministry of Refugees and Rehabilitation.

[63] Ibid., p. 102; Joseph B. Schechtman, 'Evacuee Property in India and Pakistan', *India Quarterly*, March 1953, p. 21.

[64] Ibid., p. 102.

including property deeds. By contrast, the refugees from UP and elsewhere in northern India had sufficient time to bring their property claims and other documents, facilitating early settlement in the new country. Not only were they able to reclaim urban and rural properties across Pakistan, they were also absorbed in the newly established official departments.[65] The allotment of lands, evacuee property and positions in the new government departments created better conditions.[66]

The provincial government tried to assist the refugees in the matter of evacuee property and provided all possible assistance for the allotment of lands, moveable and immovable property.

In this chapter, we have discussed the immediate post-Partition problems that Pakistan inherited, but the complex issue of arrival of refugees, reception, resettlement and rehabilitation in other areas of Pakistan, viz., West Punjab, Kashmir and East Pakistan would be analysed in the next chapter.

[65] Malik, op. cit., n. 6 above, p. 199.
[66] Ibid., p. 195.

CHAPTER 2

Pakistan and Partition Refugees in West Punjab, Kashmir and East Pakistan

As a result of the Partition of 1947, nearly seven million Indian Muslims crossed the border into (West) Pakistan. About 70 per cent of these were Punjabis who had migrated from East Punjab and settled mostly in West Punjab, which eventually absorbed 80 per cent of West Pakistan's refugee population.[1] Owing to the shared language and culture, the Punjabi immigrants assimilated rather quickly in West Punjab and ceased to identify themselves as Muhajirs. More than 4 per cent of the Urdu-speaking refugees, who were scattered in large areas of the province, also joined the Punjabi mainstream, or, at least, learnt to speak Punjabi and somehow got integrated in the new land.[2] These refugees were among the worst sufferers of the Partition holocaust.[3]

During 1946 and 1947, even before the Partition of India, serious communal disorder had erupted and widespread rioting had occurred in a number of provinces in India.[4] The Partition carnage was a free-for-all for members of all the religious communities. Hindus, Muslims and Sikhs participated in both pre- and post-

[1] Feroz Ahmed, *Ethnicity and Politics in Pakistan*, New York, Oxford, New Delhi: Oxford University Press, 1998, p. 91. For details, see Office of the Census Commissioner, *Census of Pakistan 1951*, vols. I and VI; and *Demographic Miscellany: Census Bulletin No. 6*.

[2] Ibid., p. 91.

[3] Iftikhar H. Malik, *State and Civil Society in Pakistan: Politics of Authority, Ideology and Ethnicity*, New York, London: St. Martins Press; Macmillan Press, 1977, p. 10.

[4] Keesing's Research Report 9, *Pakistan from 1947 to the Creation of Bangladesh*, New York: Charles Scribner's Sons, 1971, p. 10.

Partition orgies of violence. On the roads, in the paddy fields and on the railway tracks awaited violence, rape and death for Hindus, Muslims and Sikhs. In only three months, between August and October 1947, the whole of Punjab was seized by a communal civil war involving some of the largest campaigns of ethnic cleansing in history.[5]

Many experienced Army officers, who held the view that the carnage was a thousand times more horrible than anything they had seen during the Second World War, have described the slaughter in East Punjab. According to the best neutral sources, no fewer than 10,000 Muslims lost their lives in Amritsar district alone during August.[6] The Muslims of East Punjab were butchered in the thousands merely because of their faith.[7] The Muslim refugees who came from East to West Punjab narrated horrendous tales, which created further tension in most districts of West Punjab.

Theoretically, Pakistan and India were responsible for the protection, administration and movement of non-Muslim and Muslim refugees respectively up to the border.[8] The problems were far more numerous and onerous for Pakistan than for the Dominion of India.[9] For Pakistan, by far the most important task was to devise administrative machinery capable of performing all the functions of a modern government, and to establish this government in a new capital.[10]

The extent of the disturbance and the tremendous loss of life, and exchange of territories of lakhs of people had created unprecedented problems, which could no longer be dealt with at

[5] Syed Sikander Mehdi, 'Refugee Memory in India and Pakistan', *Transeuropéennes* (Paris), no. 19/20, Winter 2000–1, pp. 117–29.

[6] Massarat Sohail, *Partition and Anglo-Pakistan Relations 1944–51*, Lahore, Karachi, Islamabad: Vanguard Books, 1991, p. 88.

[7] Mazhar Ali Khan, *Pakistan: The First Twelve Years*, Karachi: Oxford University Press, 1996, p. 73.

[8] General Mohammad Musa Khan (retd.), *Jawan to General*, Karachi: East and West Publishing, 1984, p. 74.

[9] Chaudhri Mohammad Ali, *The Emergence of Pakistan*, Lahore: Research Society of Pakistan, University of Punjab, 1973, p. 160.

[10] Ibid., p. 161.

provincial level.[11] The problems, including division of assets, rehabilitation of refugees, and distribution of evacuee property, were aggravated when disputes arose over river waters. The occupation of Junagarh and Hyderabad by India and the war in Kashmir followed by India's threatening posture in the Punjab was a threat to Lahore.[12] India's refusal to hand over the assets amounting to over 1,000 crores due to Pakistan under the Partition Agreement gave rise to unlimited problems.[13] To overcome the problems and reduce the intensity of crises, strong, speedy and prompt measures were required.

The problems which faced the Government of Pakistan were two-fold: first, the care and resettlement of the three lakh or more refugees who had sought shelter in Pakistan; and, second, the problem of ensuring security of life and a living to those who could remain in Hindustan.[14]

Functionaries of both governments dealing with the law and order situation were frequently rendered dysfunctional and powerless before the local warlords who reigned supreme.[15]

In August, communal fighting was at a peak in the Punjab. On 16 August, Premier Liaquat Ali Khan went to Delhi to discuss the Punjab disturbance with Governor-General Mountbatten and other officials of the Indian Government.[16] Mountbatten was extremely anxious about the Sikhs. The Partition had affected the Sikhs most, and the British Government was anxious to appease them. It sent Ismay (chief of the viceroy's staff) and Mieville (the viceroy's private secretary) to hold talks with the Sikh leader, Tara Singh.[17] 'The whole country', wrote Lord Mountbatten in a letter to London a week after his arrival in India, 'is in a most unsettled state. There are communal troubles in the Punjab, NWFP, Bihar, Calcutta,

[11] Khan, op. cit., n. 7 above.

[12] Zarina Salamat, *Pakistan 1947–58: An Historical Review*, Islamabad: National Institute of Historical and Cultural Research, 1992, p. 37.

[13] Ibid., p. 35.

[14] Khan, op. cit., n. 7 above, p. 74.

[15] Mehdi, op. cit., n. 5 above, p. 120.

[16] Ali, op. cit., n. 9 above, p. 257.

[17] Salamat, op. cit., n. 12 above, p. 16.

Bombay, UP, and even here in Delhi.' The same story continued week after week, he reported to the secretary of state in the UK.

Both Prime Ministers Nehru and Liaquat Ali visited the affected areas and issued a joint statement from Amritsar on 18 August expressing their determination to suppress disorder and restore peace and security.[18] Pandit Nehru said in New Delhi that the Punjab had suffered 'untold agony at the hands of the murderers and fire raisers'. He spoke very humbly of the refugees of all communities, and declared that both himself and the Pakistani Prime Minister had decided to treat the communal problem in the Punjab as one of the first priorities to prevent violence at all costs and to protect and save the rights of the minorities on both sides of the border.[19]

By the time the transfer of power took place on 15 August, a state of virtual civil war prevailed over large portions of the Punjab. Armed gangs carried out murder, looting and arson and all communities suffered heavily.[20] The Muslim population was reported to have been virtually annihilated by Sikh *jathas* (bands armed with firearms, swords, daggers, etc.) who gave no quarter to men, women, or children. By 20 August, a mass movement of the population from the riot-affected areas of the Punjab was in full swing. It was reported from Lahore on that date out of 300,000 Hindus and Sikhs (former residents there), less than 10,000 remained, the rest having fled across the frontier to India. No reliable estimates of the number of those killed in the communal strife were available, but both the Indian and British press stated that not less than 10,000 men, women and children of all communities were murdered by the end of August.[21]

On 29 August, a high-level conference of the Joint Defence Council was held, attended by Indian and Pakistani representatives. It decided to abolish the Punjab Boundary Force (originally set up at the time of Partition to maintain law and order in the

[18] Mehdi, op. cit., n. 5 above, p. 120.

[19] Saleem Ullah Khan, *The Journey to Pakistan: A Documentation on Refugees of 1947*, Islamabad: National Documentation Centre, 1993, pp. 319–20.

[20] Keesing's, op. cit., n. 4 above, p. 10.

[21] Khan, op. cit., n. 19 above, p. 318.

disputed areas) and to replace it by new divisional headquarters, both Indian and Pakistani, which were to cooperate closely in providing guards and escorts to refugees and enable both dominions to assume direct control and responsibility of their respective territories.[22] It was also agreed that both headquarters would be situated in Lahore (Pakistan) to ensure the closest cooperation; that troops of either dominion on guard and escort duties would have the right of free passage across the frontier; that the Pakistani headquarters would be responsible for Lahore, Sialkot, Gujranwala, Sheikhupura, Lyallpur and Montgomery areas; and the Indian headquarters would have responsibility for Gurdaspur, Hoshiarpur, Jullundur, Ferozpur, Amritsar and Ludhiana areas, and for that part of Lahore district lying in India. The meeting was attended by Jinnah, Pandit Nehru, Liaquat Ali Khan, Sardar Baldev Singh, Sardar Abdul Rub Nishtar, Sir Chandulal Trivedi (Governor of East Punjab), Field Marshal Sir Claude Auchinleck (Supreme Commander, India and Pakistan), and Lieutenant-General Sir Rob Lockhart (C-in-C, Pakistan).[23]

Furthermore, concerted measures for the restoration of law and order and protection of refugees in East and West Punjab were taken up and unanimous decisions were taken at a conference held in Lahore on 3 September and attended by the premiers of both dominions.[24] Some of the decisions were as follows:

1. Both governments reiterated their determination to restore law and order immediately; to suppress and punish lawlessness; and both governments would protect all refugees and enable them to cross the border safely in both directions.
2. The East and West Punjab Governments would cooperate to the utmost in expanding the evacuations and seeing that they were carried out peacefully.
3. The East and West Punjab Governments would assume responsibility for the running of the refugee camps for both

[22] Keesing's, op. cit., n. 4 above, p. 11.
[23] Khan, op. cit., n. 19 above, p. 320.
[24] Mehdi, op. cit., n. 5 above, p. 124.

Muslims and non-Muslims in their areas, and they would provide food and other necessities equally for all refugees.

4. The evacuation from West to East Punjab and vice versa would be organized by the Indian and Pakistani military authorities with liaison officers as proper monitors being appointed by the governments in as many districts as possible to assist the refugees and maintain touch with the authorities.
5. The Governments of India and Pakistan and the provincial government agreed to declare illegal all forcible confiscation of property, not to recognize such confiscation of property, and to appoint custodians of refugees' property for agricultural lands, residential property, shops, factories, banks, insurance companies, and religious and cultural institutions.
6. Both governments would be permitted, within the limits of available transport, to take away moveable evacuee property such as personal goods, foodstuff, domestic animals, carts and other vehicles not licenced for public use, and licenced weapons.
7. Neither government would recognize forced conversions and forced marriages, and would make every effort to find and restore to their family women and girls abducted during the communal disorders.[25]

During the first week of September, the dominion Prime Minister, the Indian Defence Minister, and the Pakistan Communication Minister accompanied by ministers of the East and West Pakistan Governments extensively toured in and around the affected districts for four days,[26] and later issued a statement declaring:

> drastic action . . . taken to put down disturbances in the Punjab; armed bands would be captured and put in to concentration camps; all bands caught in the act committing crimes would be shot on sight; both governments would maintain the closest co-operation ensuring the safety and security of refugees; Muslim refugees camps would be protected by

[25] Khan, op. cit., n. 19 above, pp. 321–2.
[26] Khan, op. cit., n. 7 above, pp. 74–5.

Muslim troops and non-Muslims camps by non-Muslim troops, and that the refugees would be received, fed and rehabilitated in both dominions.[27]

Indian and Pakistani aircraft in the affected areas dropped over a lakh copies of this statement in the vernacular.

A joint statement issued by Liaquat and Nehru on 21 September affirmed that both governments were in complete agreement on the necessity to cooperate in establishing peaceful conditions, and declared:

> Any conception of conflict between India and Pakistan is repugnant not only on moral grounds but because any such conflict will result in disaster to both India and Pakistan. The two governments will therefore work to the utmost of their capacity to remove causes of conflict and to reduce as rapidly as possible both the area and intensity of the present communal conflict. In particular statements of responsible persons, which are either bellicose or one-sided, will not be permitted. It is the policy of both governments to create and maintain conditions in which minorities can live in security.[28]

It is true that both the Governments of India and of Pakistan headed respectively by Jawaharlal Nehru and Liaquat Ali Khan did work very hard to control post-Partition communal violence and cooperated extensively with each other to protect and assist the displaced.[29] During those anxious days when genocide was in progress in East Punjab and Delhi, the Pakistan Government made every effort to preserve law and order and to impress upon the people that duty and honour and the interests of Pakistan demanded peace, security, and protection for the refugees.[30]

The gigantic task of meeting all the needs of the refugees continued.[31] When the displacement started, the Government of Pakistan made an emergency committee with cabinet powers. The first meeting was held on 13 October 1947 at 10.00 a.m. It was agreed that this committee should be set up in Lahore to deal

[27] Mehdi, op. cit., n. 5 above, p. 124.

[28] Khan, op. cit., n. 19 above, pp. 323–4.

[29] Mehdi, op. cit., n. 5 above, p. 123.

[30] Ali, op. cit., n. 9 above, pp. 260–1.

[31] Ibid., p. 262.

with the refugee problem in all its aspects. This committee would be called the Pakistan-Punjab Refugees Council.[32] The Governor of West Punjab, R.F. Mudie explained different aspects of refugee-related problems in this meeting. He said that the refugee problem had three aspects:

1. the purely provincial one, for example, allotment of land for the rehabilitation of refugees;
2. the problem of inter-provincial relationships, as between West Punjab, NWFP and Sind; and
3. the international side of the question, insofar as it concerned Pakistan's relations with India.

It was, therefore, not possible to draw a sharp line between central and provincial responsibilities in this matter. It was necessary to set up a body which would work as a cabinet committee with full powers to issue orders regarding all matters relating to refugees, and maintain a proper record of its proceedings and decisions, among other things. Ultimate control was to rest with the emergency committee of the cabinet, which was to remain in constant touch with the Lahore body. The special committee was to confine itself to laying down policy in the matter of movement of refugees, their reception and rehabilitation.

The meeting was attended by the Quaid-i-Azam, Prime Minister Liaquat Ali Khan, Governor of West Punjab, R.F. Mudie, Finance Minister Ghulam Mohammad, Minister for Communication, Sardar Abdur Rub Nishtar, Minister for Interior, Information and Education Fazlur Rehman, Iftikhar Hussain Khan of Mamdat, West Punjab, Minister for Refugees & Rehabilitation, Mian Iftikhar-ud-din, Secretary to the Cabinet, Chaudhri Mohammad Ali, and Deputy Secretary to the Cabinet, S. Osman Ali.

Further, the Pakistan–West Punjab Joint Refugee and Rehabilitation Council held a meeting at Government House in Lahore on 31 October 1947. The Governments of Pakistan and West Punjab decided to set up a joint council to deal with refugees

[32] Khan, op. cit., n. 19 above, p. 5.

and rehabilitation work in West Punjab. The decision was finally ratified at this meeting.

From the start of the disturbances in West Punjab, the movement of refugees from East Punjab to West Punjab that took place till 16 September 1947 was 238,000 by rail, 254,000 on foot, and 51,500 by lorry convoys. From East Punjab to West Punjab, 245,000 came by rail, 250,160 on foot, and 60,000 by lorry convoys. The refugee movement that took place from 17 September till 5 November 1947 from East Punjab to West Punjab was 353,500 (including Muslims from Delhi and UP) by rail, 1,190,940 on foot, and 55,771 by lorry convoys. From West Punjab to East Punjab, 361,500 came by rail, 1,044,000 on foot, and 200,000 by lorry convoys. The grand total of the non-Muslims who moved out of West Punjab into India was 21.7 lakh. These figures do not include the large number of non-Muslims who moved out of West Punjab between January 1947 and 15 August 1947 during the communal disturbances.[33]

On 11 September, over 400,000 Hindu and Sikh evacuees left their homes in West Punjab and marched on foot under Indian and Pakistani military escort towards East Punjab. An official statement from Delhi announced on 16 September that the MEO had, till that date, moved about 1,000,000 refugees, of whom about 400,000 had moved from East to West Punjab and about 600,000 in the reverse direction, and Major General Chimni, head of the MEO, stated on 7 October that the evacuation was proceeding satisfactorily, with 1,628,000 refugees having already been exchanged between East and West Punjab, 450,000 still on their way, and at least 2,000,000 in West Punjab awaiting evacuation to India. The Information Bureau of the Dominion of India in New Delhi announced on 20 December that, in all, more than 8,500,000 refugees, 'the largest migration in history', had crossed the India–Pakistan border during the previous four months, of whom non-Muslims (Hindus and Sikhs) leaving Pakistan accounted for 4,362,000, and Muslims leaving India for Pakistan about 4,100,000—a movement of over 4,000,000 in each direction.[34]

[33] Ibid., pp. 1–29.

[34] Keesing's, op. cit., n. 4 above, p. 12.

The number of Muslims who moved out of East Punjab into Pakistan was 21.5 lakh. A large number of Muslims migrated to West Punjab from Amritsar, Jullundur and Gurdaspur districts in the beginning of August 1947 when the disturbance was started by Sikhs and Hindus in these districts.[35] During the four months till 10 December 1947, 4.68 million refugees had arrived in West Punjab. Of these, the MEO moved 3.92 million.[36]

By September 1947, it had become clear that only the closest cooperation between these two parallel organizations (the MEOs) could achieve the desired results. As such, the MEO (India) agreed to set up its tactical headquarters with the MEO (Pakistan) at the residency at Lahore[37] to ensure the evacuation of non-Muslim refugees from West Punjab and Muslim refugees from East Punjab. The total number of Muslim refugees moved by MEO (Pakistan) till 26 April 1948 was 36.77 lakh, and the estimated total of non-Muslim evacuees sent to India was 38.8 lakh. The figure of 38.8 lakh for the non-Muslim evacuees is as estimated by India.[38] MEO (Pakistan) organized 226 trains from Pakistan to India, and 211 train trips from India to Pakistan.[39] The evacuation of over 4,000,000 Muslim evacuees in under three and a half months was an enormous task in the face of multifarious difficulties created by the Sikhs.[40]

Evacuation work was at its peak during October 1947. Two American journalists, a man and a woman, came to the Pakistani side without previous appointment. They had come from India and enquired about the location of refugee camps on the Pakistani side and the routes along which they travelled as they intended to go and see the camps. The Pakistan Army officials briefed the journalists on these matters and provided them a station wagon to move around. The Pakistani officials told them that they should feel free to go wherever they wanted, and see anyone and whatever

[35] Khan, op. cit., n. 19 above, p. 29.

[36] Ali, op. cit., n. 9 above, p. 261.

[37] Khan, op. cit., n. 19 above, p. 58.

[38] Ibid., p. 59.

[39] Ibid., p. 60.

[40] Ibid., p. 313.

they liked. They were delighted to be allowed to have an unrestricted tour. It was unlike their experience in India, where, according to them, they were taken to a few selected places. On their return in the evening, they walked straight to the Pakistan Army office and took many photographs. Both seemed happy. The woman expressed her feelings about Pakistan's administrative machinery, and said that by giving them a free hand, Pakistan showed that it did not feel guilty and had nothing to hide, and looked after the non-Muslim refugees better than the Indians did. They appeared to be particularly impressed by the Pakistan Government's concern regarding evacuation of refugees.[41] On 15 December, the MEO (Pakistan) set up a special 'pocket clearance' organization, and from the beginning of January, most of the evacuation work concentrated on such pockets of converted persons and abducted women. The actual number of Muslims who had entered West Punjab till 10 March 1948, according to the West Punjab Refugees Census, was 5,486,979. However, the period during which the greatest movement occurred was from September to December 1947, both months inclusive. A considerable number of refugees were sent to Sind in order to ease West Punjab's rehabilitation problem.[42]

The Pakistan Government along with the Punjab Council had rendered great efforts for the evacuation of Muslims and non-Muslims and provided all possible facilities including motor transport, trains, lorries, etc. Pakistan had received the refugees with great enthusiasm and the warmest welcome.

The mass movement of over 8,000,000 refugees had created resettlement and rehabilitation problems of the greatest magnitude both in India and Pakistan.[43] Migration had started on 11 August 1947, when refugees from Amritsar district began to pour into Lahore and other places in very large numbers. At first, the Boy Scouts Headquarters (Camp No. I) was opened. It was run by a large Boy Scout staff. This camp overflowed within a few days,

[41] Khan, op. cit., n. 8 above, p. 82.

[42] Khan, op. cit., n. 19 above, p. 60.

[43] Keesing's, op. cit., n. 4 above, p. 13.

and Walton (Camp No. II) had to be opened. Soon, the third camp (Camp No. III) had to be opened at Walton on 1 September.[44]

These camps were administered at first by an officer directly responsible to the provincial government, and later to the joint secretariat of the Pakistan Punjab Refugees Council. Along with these, a large number of refugee and evacuee camps were opened by the deputy commissioners, as the refugees moved to different parts of West Punjab or as the evacuees decided to depart. A number of other camps were opened by the district authorities at Kasur, Wagha, Hudiara, Bowli, Sulemanki and Shahadara to deal with the mass of refugees fleeing on foot to West Punjab, and were also taken under the direct administration of the council. Adequate trained staff was provided for each camp, and arrangements initiated to run them according to plan.

A scheme of management of camps was drawn up giving detailed instructions for the treatment of refugees at each stage of their sojourn in camps from the time of entry to that of departure, providing especially for reception, issue of rations and clothing, census, information, recording complaints of abduction and loss of property, etc.

The camps were divided from A to E blocks, each block accommodating about 7,000. Each had different offices. In the first office, a certificate indicating that the bearer was a genuine refugee was given. In the second office, refugees were asked to record their lost property, relatives, and others; the third office was known as an enquiry office, where refugees could obtain all sorts of information about their relatives in the camps.

The Walton group of camps—Walton Scouts School, Chinese Barrack and Civil Aerodrome—were maintained by the government at an average cost of Rs. 30,000 a day and accommodated 130,000 persons at a time. There were 200 officers, including a chief camp superintendent, assisted by three superintendents and many assistants, superintendents, barracks officers and volunteers. Many offices were set up in the camp to deal with various problems such as reception, education, food, dispersal, transportation,

[44] Khan, op. cit., n. 19 above, p. 41.

registration, burial, and other needs. Special attention was paid to food supplies. The transport facilities were not adequate to supply wheat and other things. The district authorities used to make arrangements for the supply of food to refugees in their districts. Efforts were made to bring these arrangements up to the standard of the centrally-managed administration-approved ration scale and by issuing tinned milk throughout the province. Besides, large quantities of cooked food donated by the people of Lahore used to be transported to the camps.

At Wagha, a constant supply of *atta*, rice and *dal*, was ensured since the camps were set up. The average daily consumption was 200 bags of *atta*, 10 bags of *dal*, and 50 bags of rice. The refugees generally arrived in these camps in starved condition. Food for 10,000 people was always kept ready at Walton because it was the main transit camp. In December, the government also agreed to provide fodder for the cattle belonging to refugees up to the resettlement stage at a cost of approximately Re. 1 per bullock per day.

It was also decided to keep as large a number of refugees in the camps in Lahore, because provision for shelter and supervision were easier here. The Lahore camps had about 235,000 refugees. Special arrangements were made in the districts to put up shelters where alternative accommodation was not available, and *sarkanda* huts and other temporary structures were put up to house refugees.

Large numbers of refugees had been stripped of the greater part of their belongings and most of them had escaped with only the clothes they were wearing. The clothing problem had, therefore, become very important, specially with the onset of the cold weather. Fairly satisfactory arrangements were made, and large quantities of warm clothing distributed and cotton clothing, blankets, *razais* and bedding given to the refugees through the Quaid-i-Azam's Relief Fund.[45]

A number of new winter camps were also opened throughout West Punjab. This step was taken to save the refugees from the rigours of the cold weather. The Ministry of Refugees issued

[45] Ibid., pp. 41–62, 271–8.

instructions regarding the winter camps.[46] On 5 October, an appeal was issued by Prime Minister Liaquat Ali Khan to foreign countries for warm clothes for refugees. He said, 'Two and a half million Muslim refugees will shortly have to face the rigors of Western Pakistan winter. It is of the utmost importance that they be provided with warm clothing and blankets.' At that time, Pakistan didn't have a single woollen mill. Gifts of warm clothing, among other necessary items, were of immense value when dispatched to the camps.[47]

The Deputy Commissioner, Lahore, inaugurated a 'Quilt Week', yielding a very welcome 35,000 quilts for the refugees. The government also prepared and distributed up to 10,000 quilts. In addition, the Civil Supplies Department reserved West Punjab's quota of cloth exclusively for refugees.

A very high proportion of refugees were wounded, exhausted or suffering from ailments because most of them came to West Punjab after prolonged stay at the camps. In these camps, they contracted diseases and had to undergo slow starvation. Provision of proper medical attention was of utmost importance for them. Satisfactory arrangements were made as the issue at all the centrally managed camps. The Ministry of Refugees itself was immediately concerned with the question of voluntary aid. A total of 8 doctors, 4 nurses, and 16 administrative officers (for the most part, ex-army officers or civilians who had seen service in the subcontinent) were recruited by Pakistan's High Commissioner in the UK and sent out by air to Pakistan, or were recruited locally by the ministry. Besides these, voluntary missionary societies, particularly in the UK and US, also sent their members to Pakistan. The Society of Friends also sent medical units. The Christian Committee for Relief in West Pakistan accepted responsibility for general administrative control of all volunteer aid. Volunteer administrative officers were detailed to help in administration of the camps. These volunteers performed service of great value. Funds for the maintenance of these volunteers were made available from the Quaid-i-Azam's Relief Fund.

[46] Ibid., p. 297.

[47] Ibid., p. 265.

In October 1947, the Governor of West Punjab issued an appeal through the columns of the *Times* in London for volunteer workers who were willing to come to Pakistan to help the administration with the refugees relief problem. Special efforts were made under the guidance of the Governor of West Punjab to keep up the morale of the refugees. Schools were opened for both children and adults, and the number of students steadily increased.

Scouting and girl guiding was introduced in most of the camps and the movement gained headway. The adults were given drill and physical training and all inmates of camps were provided facilities for games and sports with weekly competitions between different blocks. There were schools for industrial training and provision was made to enable those passing out of them to take a set of tools with them. In the evening, lectures, cinema shows and singing competitions, were held. All these efforts boosted the morale of the refugees. The Quaid-i-Azam's Relief Fund granted Rs. 8 lakh for this purpose.

He emphasized the need for assistance to refugees. Addressing the people of Pakistan, he said:

> Create enthusiasm and spirit and go forward with our task with courage and hope. We shall do it. Are we down hearted? Certainly not. The history of Islam is replete with instance of valour, grit and determination. So march on notwithstanding obstructions, obstacles and interference and I feel confident that a gifted nation of 70 million people need grim determination and with great civilization and history, need fear nothing. It is now up to you to work, work and work and we are bound to succeed and do not forget our motto, Unity, Discipline and Faith.[48]

On both sides of the Punjab frontier, entire villages and large areas of productive land were left abandoned by the former occupants, while in the towns and cities, such as Lahore and Multan, many shops and businesses became defunct through the emigration of their owners to the other dominion.[49] As time passed, lands, factories and shops available to new arrivals began to diminish.[50] Both the East and West Punjab provincial governments made

[48] Ibid., pp. 44–66, 240.

[49] Keesing's, op. cit., n. 4 above, p. 13.

[50] Ali, op. cit., n. 9 above, p. 264.

intensive efforts to resettle the new immigrant population on the lands vacated by the emigrants.[51] Besides this, Sir Francis Mudie, Governor of West Punjab, and government servants of all ranks worked devotedly and enthusiastically day and night to diminish the magnitude of the problems.

Loans for agricultural operations were given to the refugees settling on the land. To aid refugee artisans, the Refugees Rehabilitation Finance Corporation with a capital of Rs. 30 million was set up. An endeavour was made to settle artisans in special colonies.[52] Agriculturalist Muslim refugees were rehabilitated on crown land in the canal colonies as well as on lands vacated by the Hindus and Sikhs. In West Punjab, 8-acre plots of land were allotted to the refugees,[53] while Sind received nearly double this area.[54] There were many village artisans who lost their employment because they had lost their tools or were unable to start work because of the absence of necessary small capital.[55] To mitigate this problem, the government made praiseworthy efforts. The refugees who were allotted land received grants to buy agricultural equipment and seeds.[56]

The most dramatic aspect of rehabilitation was the recovery of abducted women and converts, a very important activity, which continued for several months. As the movement of refugees continued over a period of weeks and months, it became increasingly clear that large numbers of women and children were left behind on either side. An inter-dominion conference was, therefore, called on 6 December, and it was decided that the work of rescuing these women and children and also evacuating converts from 'pockets' should be carried out in right earnest.[57]

[51] Keesing's, op. cit., n. 4 above, p. 13.

[52] Ali, op. cit., n. 9 above, pp. 266–7.

[53] Mudie to Jinnah, 19 April 1948, Mudie Papers, Mss. Eur. F 164/15, IOR referred to in Ian Talbot, *Freedom's Cry, The Popular Dimension in the Pakistan Movement and Partition Experience in North-West India*, Karachi: Oxford University Press, 1996, p. 173.

[54] Ibid., p. 173.

[55] Khan, op. cit., n. 19 above, p. 47.

[56] Talbot, *Freedom*, op. cit., n. 78 above, p. 174.

[57] Khan, op. cit., n. 19 above, p. 61.

In fact, inter-dominion cooperation was more successful when it came to the recovery of abducted women and children. Recovery offices and transit camps were set up in both countries following the agreement in November 1948.[58] A special organization was established for this purpose; counselling services were also provided to the victims. After a lot of hard work spread over a period of months, 6,355 Muslim women were recovered and an approximately equal number of non-Muslim women, including those recovered from the Azad Kashmir Government's territory, were transferred to India.[59] By October 1952, over 8,000 abducted women and children were shifted from Pakistan to India. Twice this number of Muslim women and children were recovered from India.[60]

The trouble in Kashmir started in August 1947, when the Hindu Maharaja, Sir Hari Singh, started applying the same techniques of brutality to the Muslim population as were being employed by the Sikh and Hindu rulers of the princely states of Kapurthala, Faridkot, Patiala, Nabha, Alwar and Gwalior.[61] The fate of Kashmir in 1947 was symbolically significant for both Pakistan and India. As a Muslim-majority princely state, it was expected that it would join Pakistan after the lapse of British paramountcy. But its non-inclusion not only created disturbance for the people of Kashmir, but also threatened the ideological basis of Pakistan's existence.[62] In August 1947, an anti-Muslim movement within the state was initiated with all the appearance of a systematic persecution. It started on 26 August at Bagh in Poonch.[63] In Poonch and Mirpur, populated by a thousand demobilized soldiers of the Second World War, in order to assert Dogra rule, the Maharaja's armies wantonly plundered the areas inhabited by Muslims and set fire to their

[58] Ali, op. cit., p. 274, referred to in Talbot, op. cit., n. 78 above, p. 173.

[59] Khan, op. cit., n. 19 above, p. 61.

[60] Ali, op. cit., p. 274, referred to in Talbot, op. cit., n. 78 above, p. 173.

[61] G.W. Choudhary, *Pakistan's Relations with India 1947–1966*, London: Pall Mall Press, 1968, p. 92.

[62] Ian Talbot, *Pakistan: A Modern History*, Karachi, Lahore, Islamabad: Vanguard Books, 1999, p. 114.

[63] Choudhary, op. cit., n. 61 above, p. 93.

homes. The government wanted to massacre people (Muslims) without letting the world know what was going on.[64] This continued, and increased in tempo with the infiltration of members of the RSS, Akali Sikhs and the Indian National Army (INA), and in Jammu province in October, where Hindus and Sikhs slightly outnumbered the Muslims, the Maharaja's plan of extermination had its main success. 'Within a period of eleven weeks starting in August 1947', writes Ian Stephens, 'systematic savageries, similar to those already launched in East Punjab, Patiala, Kapurthala, practically eliminated the entire Muslim element in the population, amounting to 5,00,000 people. About 2,00,000 just disappeared, remaining untraceable, having presumably been butchered or died from epidemics or exposure.' The *Times* wrote on 10 October 1947: '237,000 Muslims were intentionally exterminated (unless they escaped to Pakistan) by Dogra forces, headed by the Maharaja in person.'[65]

The September 1947 communal massacre in Jammu and Poonch pushed over 80,000 Muslim refugees to West Pakistan.[66] The Central Ministry of Refugees estimated that the refugee influx to West Punjab was 52.78 lakh, plus 2.5 lakh from Kashmir (Jammu refugees).[67]

The plight of Kashmiri refugees was just as pitiable as that of those who arrived in Lahore from Indian Punjab. They were subjected to similar brutalities. Many men, women and children had their bodies mutilated. The number of those who had suffered injuries was countless.[68] First, Pakistan had to arrange camps for their settlement, and provide medical facilities for the suffering refugees. It was also concerned for the security of these refugees. Pakistan also protested against the brutalities of the Indian state in the overwhelmingly Muslim state of Kashmir.

Prime Minister Liaquat Ali Khan, for instance, sent a telegram to the British Prime Minister on 29 October 1947: 'There is no

[64] Ibid., p. 173.
[65] Ibid., pp. 93–4.
[66] Talbot, op. cit., n. 53 above, p. 116 .
[67] Khan, op. cit., n. 19 above, p. 55.
[68] Musa, op. cit., n. 8 above, pp. 86–7.

doubt that the state troops attacked Muslims at Poonch, women and children took refuge in Pakistan, and burning villages could be seen from our border . . . later they set out to massacre Muslims of Jammu.' Liaquat further revealed that the Dogra Brigadier in command of Jammu had admitted that his orders were to drive out Muslims from a belt of territory three miles wide.[69] When the American military attaché visited Pakistan, the Pakistani authorities arranged his tour of refugee camps. For a moment, he stood aghast at the terrible sight in the camp and cursed the people concerned for their cruelty. The Pakistani Brigade Commander Mohammad Musa requested the attaché to bring the evidence of Indian misdeeds which he had seen with his own eyes to the notice of his government and his colleagues in Pakistan. The military attaché took many photographs, which he said he would send to America with his report on his visit to the camp.[70]

The government functionaries received the mass of refugees with commendable efficiency. The refugee problem stretched government resources to the breaking point. It was a gigantic task to move to the interior to care for the incoming Kashmiri refugees.[71]

Physically almost wrecked and mentally disturbed, the refugees from Kashmir continued pouring in, asking for shelter and rehabilitation. Due attention was paid to food supply and provision of medical aid to the sufferers in adequate quantities and in time. In the American Missionary Hospital at Sialkot, hundreds of injured women and children were sent for medical aid. In addition to the civilians, the Pakistan Army played a memorable role in assisting these Kashmiris.

The Pakistan Army tackled the situation very efficiently. Of course, it was by no means perfect, but the Pakistan Army, which was not yet properly organized, rushed to rescue and provide relief to the helpless refugees, who were preyed upon by armed hooligans. Soon, the Army took over the administration of the refugee camps

[69] Ibid., p. 95.
[70] Musa, op. cit., n. 8 above, p. 87.
[71] Ibid., pp. 85–7.

from civil authorities as the resources of the latter could not ensure the supply of food and medical aid in time. The main problem was to bring the refugees from border areas as safely as possible. There was paucity of troops for the numerous jobs, but a few units worked around the clock and carried out a Herculean task with commendable devotion and efficiency. Most of the time, the soldiers moved along with the convoys headed for Pakistan, protected them at night, and shared their Army rations with half-starved people.

The Indian military and civil armed forces raided some of the villages along the Sialkot–Jammu border off and on. They did so to prevent the Pakistani people from raiding their territory. They also attacked the vehicle convoys on the Kahuta–Jammu road and attempted to force the Pakistani villagers out of their homes to create a no-man's land on the Pakistani side of the frontier. On 13 November, a heavily armed mob supported by the Jammu state military attacked Dhangi village in Sialkot district. It was confronted by West Punjab home guards. Near the Gujrat–Jammu border, a mob of about 1,000 (including military men), from Jammu state attacked Muslims working in their fields on the Pakistan side of the border. The Pakistan military men, however, came to their rescue in time and put the raiders to flight after inflicting 20 casualties on them.[72] The Muslims of India and of the State of Jammu and Kashmir were made the victims of a deliberately planned genocide, with the intention of undoing Pakistan at its birth,[73] but Pakistan welcomed the Muhajirs with great generosity and wholeheartedly helped them in their rehabilitation.

The 1946 massacre of Muslims in Bihar was the first organized effort at extermination of opponents over a wide area.[74] The story of Bihari refugees is one of colossal bad fortunes even for this part of the world.[75] The Muslims of Bombay, UP and Bihar were the first to respond to the call of Jinnah for Partition, and enthu-

[72] Khan, op. cit., n. 19 above, p. 302.

[73] Musa, op. cit., n. 8 above, p. 88.

[74] Ali, op. cit., n. 9 above, p. 254.

[75] Mushtaq Naqvi, *Partition, The Real Story*, New Delhi: Renaissance Publishing, 1995, p. 124.

siastically supported the movement for Pakistan and became its vanguard.[76]

The Biharis, comprising Muslim immigrants from Bihar and parts of UP and Rajasthan,[77] came from the neighbouring Hindu-majority provinces of Rajasthan, Madhya Pradesh and Bihar,[78] and went to East Bengal at the time of Independence.[79]

Their displacement occurred in the wake of communal violence, when the Hindu attacks on Muslims in Bihar started in Patna on 26 October 1946, several months before Partition. It soon spread throughout Monghyr district, and within one month, over 100,000 people suffered displacement. Despite British efforts, many refugees refused to go back to their villages from the camps in which they were housed.[80] By the end of November, more than 400 Muslims had crossed the provincial boundary and taken shelter in Bengal.[81] In the great Bihar killing, approximately 30,000 Muslims were massacred. About a million of them migrated to the eastern wing of Pakistan (East Pakistan)[82] between August and November 1947. At the same time, an equal number of Hindus and Sikhs had departed for India.[83]

Initially, camps were set up for Bihari refugees in East Pakistan. Government functionaries, along with the International Committee of the Red Cross (ICRC), had rendered all possible support in terms of refugee rehabilitation. During the period of united Pakistan (1947–71), the Urdu-speaking Biharis could not assimilate with the society of East Pakistan and remained a distinct cultural-linguistic group. They generally identified themselves with the West Pakistani society, partly because of a shared linguistic heritage, and supported the West Pakistani governing elite in its scramble for

[76] Rafiq Zakaria, *The Man Who Divided India, An Insight into Jinnah's Leadership and its Aftermath*, Mumbai: Popular Prakashan, 2001, p. 202.

[77] Ibid., p. 201.

[78] Ibid., p. 213.

[79] Naqvi, op. cit., n. 79 above, p. 125.

[80] Talbot, op. cit., n. 53 above, pp. 156–7.

[81] Mehdi, op. cit., n. 5 above, p. 119.

[82] www.refugee watch/www.safhr.org/refugees

[83] Talbot, op. cit., n. 62 above, p. 101.

economic and political power in East Pakistan. The Biharis, consequently, enjoyed government patronage and preferential treatment in various sectors. Their attachment to north Indian culture led to increasing conflict with the indigenous Bengali elite. In March 1948, when Mohammed Ali Jinnah, the founder of the Pakistani state announced in Dhaka that 'Urdu and Urdu alone shall be the state language of Pakistan', the Bengalis launched the language movement in support of their mother tongue, Bengali. The Biharis, instead of supporting the Bengalis, sided with the West Pakistani ruling elite. Further, in the 1954 provincial elections and in the 1970 general elections, the Biharis extended their support to the West Pakistan–based Muslim League, which symbolized and championed the domination of West Pakistan over Bengalis.[84] In 1971, following a bloody struggle for independence, East Pakistan became Bangladesh. The Biharis were loyal to Pakistan. They actively participated in the military action against the Bengalis in East Pakistan and supported the West Pakistan ruling elite. Because of their active anti-independence role, the Biharis were subjected to widespread political persecution before, during, and after the war of liberation launched by the Bengalis in 1971.

When the Punjabi-dominated Pakistan Army was defeated and Bangladesh came into existence as an independent country, the Biharis were the first targets of Bengali freedom fighters.[85] Thousands were killed as traitors and hundreds of thousands were uprooted.[86] The Bengalis unleashed a war of retribution throughout the country. Matiur Rehman and Naeem Hasan, in their book *Iron Bars of Freedom*, describe how, within hours of the surrender of Dacca to the Indian Army, the Bengali freedom fighters ran amuck and took revenge: 'The planned cold-blooded killings that followed and which resulted in the loss of thousands of lives . . . the victims were unarmed civilians, Biharis and the vanquished paramilitary personnel . . . thousands were lynched, flogged, flayed,

[84] Refugee Watch/www.safhr.org/refugee

[85] Zakaria, op. cit., n. 80 above, p. 214.

[86] Naqvi, op. cit., n. 79 above, p. 125.

mutilated, cleaved and butchered because they had chosen to stay loyal to their erstwhile state—Pakistan.'[87]

The persecution of Biharis continued and their properties and houses were plundered by the Bengalis. They were deprived of their belongings, possessions, and jobs. They were utterly helpless and dispossessed.

Some Biharis managed to migrate from Bangladesh to Pakistan after the conflict, but most were too poor to make the move. The residual population remained stranded in Bangladesh.[88] The people in the squalid shanty town of Geneva camp counted themselves among the world's most unwanted refugees.[89] They had rejected Bangladeshi citizenship, and Pakistan was not willing to take them back. The Biharis looked to Pakistan for assistance. About 170,000 Biharis were repatriated to Pakistan with the help of the International Red Cross. Pakistan then expressed its reluctance to take more. Its great reluctance was because of the huge cost of large-scale resettlement and out of fear that the Biharis' arrival could exacerbate existing ethnic and political tensions in Pakistan.[90]

These Biharis are an unwanted and harassed lot in Bangladesh. They are eager to go to Pakistan. In a generation, they fled two homelands and then discovered that Pakistan was unwilling to accept the remaining 250,000 of its nationals stranded in Bangladesh. The Biharis continue to live in refugee-like circumstances in the camps in Bangladesh, even though many still fly Pakistani flags on top of their tents and request the Pakistani authorities to rescue them and give them shelter in any small corner of Pakistan.

Conditions in the Biharis' camps are terrible: sanitation and water supply are inadequate. Naked and partially-clothed children plough through the mud and fly-infected sewage ditches.[91] Crime is also a problem, and sex traffickers reportedly target young Bihari women.[92]

[87] Zakaria, op. cit., n. 76 above, p. 215.
[88] www.refugees.org/world/article
[89] Naqvi, op. cit., n. 75 above, p. 124.
[90] www.refugees.org/world/article
[91] Naqvi, op. cit., n. 75 above, p. 124.
[92] www.refugees.org/world/article

The Bangladesh Government announced Presidential Order 149 in 1972 as a step towards offering Bangladeshi citizenship to the Biharis. According to Bangladesh Government sources, some 600,000 Biharis accepted the offer,[93] while 539,669 registered themselves with the ICRC and opted to return to their country of nationality, Pakistan. But Islamabad showed little interest and had a lax attitude to the repatriation of Biharis. What is most pitiable is the fact that several Pakistani governments did express sympathy with their plight, but no one did anything to diminish the sufferings of the Biharis despite offers of financial assistance from Saudi Arabia and several other Muslim countries.

No Pakistani ruler, civilian or military, whether Bhutto, Zia, Benazir, Sharif or Musharraf, has done enough to rehabilitate the Biharis in Pakistan or alleviate their suffering. No religious or secular organization in Pakistan has came forward to alleviate their sufferings. None of them, whether the devout Muslims of Sind, Punjab, the Frontier or Baluchistan extended a helping hand and provided them some kind of home somewhere in Pakistan.[94] But the August 2002 visit of Pakistan President General Pervez Musharraf to Bangladesh sparked hopes among Biharis. However, while Musharraf and Bangladeshi Prime Minister Khaleda Zia reportedly discussed the issue of Biharis, no progress was made, and the Bangladeshis continued to demand their relocation to Pakistan.[95]

In the light of the discussion above on the refugee exodus to Pakistan from Indian Punjab and the state of Jammu and Kashmir, one may confidently conclude that the early history of Pakistan is an impressive saga of courage and positivity that any people can be proud of. It was a colossal task of hosting the waves of physically and mentally wrecked sufferers. The new state had begun from scratch. The government performed its responsibilities with com-

[93] Ministry of Relief and Rehabilitation, Government of the People's Republic of Bangladesh, *Stranded Pakistanis in Bangladesh*, Dhaka: Government of Bangladesh, 1982, p. 3, cited in Refugee Watch: www.safhr.org/refugee

[94] Zakaria, op. cit., n. 76 above, p. 216.

[95] www.refugees.org/world/article

mendable efficiency and provided all possible assistance to those who were uprooted from their ancestral homes and were pushed across the border under terrifying circumstances. The way the government rushed to their rescue and saved their lives and honour is a glorious chapter in the early history of Pakistan. However, this early history has been tarnished to a great extent by two major developments in later years. They are Pakistan's total disregard to the plight of the Biharis in Bangladesh, and the state's growing discrimination against Partition refugees in post-1958 Sind province in Pakistan.

The next chapter aims at discussing the political, economic, and social developments in Pakistan, and the decline of power and influence of the Partition refugees.

CHAPTER 3

Post-1958 Pakistan and Partition Refugees in Sind

This chapter deals with the political, economic, and social developments in Pakistan since the advent of the military regime of General Ayub Khan and the gradual decline of the political, governmental and economic power and influence of the Partition refugees.

The first decade of Pakistan (1947–57) was doubtless a chaotic one when the newly independent country had to face enormous economic, security, administrative and financial challenges. It also had to bear the consequences of bad governance, political intrigues, undemocratic traditions, frequent rise and fall of governments, lack of direction and lack of concern for long-term planning. One may just go on enumerating the failures of the new state, but there is the other side of the picture too. The state successfully dealt with the challenge of the Partition carnage and the issue of the Partition refugees.

As explained in the earlier chapters, during the first decade of its existence, Pakistan did quite well in handling the Partition refugee issue. The task clearly was easier to handle in the Punjab. Most of the refugees coming from Indian Punjab were Punjabis. They spoke the same language, had the same culture, and their integration was easy. Of course, they were the worst victims of the Partition carnage, but their resettlement was smooth and rapid.

The task of resettlement was far more challenging in Sind where the refugees from India had migrated to start a new life. It was a different environment. The people of Sind spoke Sindhi, and the refugees generally spoke Urdu. The Sindhi culture was somewhat different. Even though the Sindhis received these Partition refugees with open arms, the post-Partition euphoria was to die down soon. These Indian refugees had almost taken the city of Karachi by storm. They were now spreading out in the other urban centres of Sind. They were in the government, in the All Pakistan Muslim League, the bureaucracy, and in business. They were becoming a threat to the traditional institutions of power in the territories of Pakistan: feudalism, tribalism, and the military.

The military takeover of Pakistan under the leadership of General Ayub Khan in October 1958 pronounced the beginning of a new relationship between the Pakistani State and the Partition refugees. The State was now determined to diminish the political and economic power of these refugees. This was one way of ensuring the supremacy of feudalism, tribalism, and military power in the country.

On the eve of Partition, the total number of Indian Muslims was around 100 million, out of whom 65 million became Pakistani nationals and the rest 35–40 million remained in India.[1] Karachi, Hyderabad, Lyallpur, and Sargodha had refugees as 60 per cent of their population. Being the federal capital from 1947 to 1958 and being Jinnah's city, Karachi especially attracted a large number of Indian refugees.

As a matter of fact, during the first decade of Pakistan existence (1947–58), Karachi had remained the centre of political and economic activity. It was also the fertile breeding ground of democratic activism. The refugees coming to Karachi were gradually integrated with this ever-expanding city. They also felt empowered and played an important role in the development of the city. They joined the bureaucracy, judiciary, police, Armed Forces, businesses and the emerging civil society. Since many of them came from very advanced centres of learning and many had actively participated in political struggles and civil society struggles, they also

[1] Iftikhar H. Malik, *State and Civil Society in Pakistan: Politics of Authority, Ideology and Ethnicity*, New York, London: St. Martins Press; Macmillan Press, 1997, p. 199. For details, see *Census of India*, 1941, Command No. 6479, Tables II and VI.

actively contributed to the growth of political culture in Karachi and Pakistan.

In many ways, however, the Muhajir culture, in most of its important manifestations, was different from the indigenous culture of Pakistan. The refugees and the indigenous leadership were products of two very different political cultures. A clash between them was inevitable.[2] The Muhajir elite generally desired a clear separation of religion and State, but there was a strong element in the indigenous leadership which preferred the system in conformity with the dictates of the Koran and Sunna and advocated firm interconnectedness between politics and religion. Divergence also existed on economic issues. The Muhajirs believed in secularism, liberal politics, laissez-faire economics and could not agree to a federal and tribal set-up, but the native feudals and tribal influential were all for this set-up. Differences also developed over political issues.

The first clash occurred over the question of organizing the Muslim League, the party which had won the battle for Pakistan under the leadership of Mohammed Ali Jinnah. The Partition refugees gained important positions in the party and in the cabinet. The second clash came over the question of writing a constitution for the new country, and this clash was mainly between the Muhajir leadership and the landed aristocracy and religious leadership. Ultimately, the feudal leadership under the aegis of the military emerged triumphant.

The feudals really had an upper hand in Pakistan's politics ever since the military regime came to power in Pakistan in October 1958. The event was not welcomed by the Muhajirs. The dwellers of Karachi were clearly in favour of leaders like Jinnah, Liaquat, Fatima Jinnah and others, and were ready to fight against the military regime of Ayub Khan to protect Jinnah's secular, democratic and modernistic Pakistan and Karachi. But the realization was slow to emerge that the long reign of Ayub would eventually result in the eclipse of the Muhajirs' positions of primacy and influence in politics, bureaucracy, and business.

[2] Shahid Javed Burki, *Pakistan: Fifty Years of Nationhood*, Lahore: Vanguard Books, 1999, p. 28.

Ayub's rule really benefited the Punjabis and Pathans a lot. After the coup in 1958, all power got concentrated in the hands of the military: the Punjabis dominated this institution. The Punjabis were the major beneficiaries of Ayub's rule, and their domination in the civil bureaucracy also increased with the passage of time. The Ayubian drive for modernization and rapid industrial development also helped the emergence of the Punjabi capitalist class.

Here we may refer to Hamza Alavi's (1973) notion of an overdeveloped State. The notion largely derived from Alavi's analysis of the Pakistani State of the 1960s. He argues that a predominantly Punjabi military bureaucracy dominated Pakistan in the 1960s. Worse still, the Punjabi ethno-centricity failed to structurally assimilate or politically integrate other ethnic groups.[3]

Sometimes, the particularistic state structure, authoritarianism and inter-regional imbalances together with uneven development in line with the major demographic changes caused by immigration led to increased tension in the polity.[4] After the 1958 coup, the tension increased. The very fact of the predominantly Punjabi military directly assuming political power meant, at the very least, a curtailment in the power of the civilian bureaucracy and the power of the Muhajirs. Many of the top functionaries in the Ayub regime were Muhajirs. The new trend was to convert the Muhajirs from senior partners to junior partners or to get rid of them from important positions. The trend was reflected in Sind as well, where the Muhajirs had retained an overall numerical domination in relation to Sindhis in government offices, but they gradually lost many positions to the Punjabis, specially at the higher level.

During 1955–70, in Hyderabad and Khairpur divisions, of the 90 individuals who served as deputy commissioners (district administrators/magistrates), 51 were Muhajirs, 25 Sindhis, and 14 were Punjabis. Similarly, in the police, for the post of superintendent of police (district police chief), 64 were held by Muhajirs out of 159, vis-à-vis 51 by Sindhis and 44 by Punjabis. At the divisional

[3] Uma Singh, 'Ethnic Conflicts', in *Political System of Pakistan: Political Parties, Election and Regionalism*, ed. Verinder Grover and Ranjana Arora, New Delhi: Deep and Deep, 1995, p. 521.

[4] Malik, op. cit., n. 1 above, p. 181.

level, of the 17 persons who served as commissioners, 9 were Muhajirs, 8 Punjabis, and one Sindhi, while of the 20 persons who were posted as deputy inspectors general of police, 12 were Punjabis, 6 Muhajirs, and 2 Sindhis. In Karachi also, increasing numbers of Punjabis were being posted as commissioners and deputy commissioners, while the Punjabis and Pathans were rapidly replacing the Muhajirs in the police (*Paligo*, 1990).

It was not easy to rise and protest against Ayub's moves. Ayub had also moved quickly on several different fronts. The imposition of martial law had brought a whole series of repressive measures abolishing all civil liberties, censoring the press, and imposing extraordinary penalties for criminal acts. Special military courts were established and authorized to pass any sentence 'except death, transportation or imprisonment exceeding one year or whipping exceeding fifteen stripes'.[5] Several prominent members of the previous regime were arrested and held without bail. Others were confined to their homes. Early in 1959, the Public Conduct Offices (Disqualification) Order, 1959, was promulgated.[6] Special tribunals were established to try former political leaders.

Ayub Khan believed that developing nations needed economic development, political stability and unity more than any other thing. He held the view that a nation needed to attain a sufficient level of economic development first, and that liberal democratic institutions were unnecessary because these would only divide people and encourage disintegrative forces.[7]

As for industrialization, in the virtual absence of a Pakistani class of industrialists it was only the ruling bureaucracy that began to promote it in the 1950s, maintaining that Pakistan would not be economically viable without an industrial base. A bureaucratic-military oligarchy soon emerged and became the new governing class.[8] It usurped state power almost unnoticed. The new

[5] Karl Von Vorys, *Political Developments in Pakistan*, London and Karachi: Princeton University Press, 1965, p. 189.

[6] Ibid.

[7] Hasan Askari Rizvi, *The Military 1947–86 and Politics in Pakistan*, Lahore: Progressive Publishers, 1986, p. 102.

[8] Hamza Alavi, 'Building Blocks of the New Pakistani State', *Daily Dawn* (Karachi), 23 March 2003.

industrialists included members of Ayub's immediate family. The President insisted that there was nothing wrong in this.[9] Ayub allowed his sons to leave the Army and enter industry.[10] The relationship between the government and business altered drastically, and the business class became more active, more sophisticated, and soon penetrated all social sectors, owned newspapers, and financed political groups. Their support meant a lot in politics. Inter-marriage between leading industrial families and families of civil servants became commonplace. While rapid industrialization created a number of white-collar jobs for Punjabi- and Urdu-speaking educated people, it allured the Punjabis and Pathans, specially from rural Punjab and NWFP, to come down to Karachi, work in the factories and constitute a powerful non-Muhajir working class in Karachi. This had considerable implications for the second-generation Partition refugees and for the city of Karachi as well.

Soon after coming to power in 1958, General Ayub Khan announced land reforms relating to the ownership and tenancy of agricultural land and for ensuring better production and social justice as well as security of tenure for those engaged in cultivation.[11]

The reforms were accompanied by a drive to introduce modern methods of farming, use of better seeds, better credit facilities, and improvement in market conditions.[12] In reality, however, the reforms were mismanaged, and it is alleged that nearly 10 million acres of land were awarded to retired army personnel, mostly Punjabis, who went to rural Sind as farmers.[13]

According to reports, in 1956, virgin lands were given to Punjabi civilian and military bureaucrats, and by 1960 about two-thirds of the land of the province of Sind had been assigned to either Urdu-

[9] Lawrence Ziring, *The Ayub Khan Era: Politics in Pakistan 1958–69*, New York: Syracuse University Press, 1971, p. 88. For details, see Gustav F. Papnek, *Pakistan's Development, Social Goals and Private Incentives*, Cambridge: Harvard University Press, 1967, p. 10.

[10] Burki, op. cit., n. 2 above, p. 37.

[11] Government of West Pakistan, *Land Reforms Commission for West Pakistan*, Lahore: Government of West Pakistan, 1959.

[12] Ibid., p. 98.

[13] Singh, op. cit., n. 3 above, p. 517.

speaking claimants or Punjabi settlers.[14] A number of senior officers were permitted to acquire large portions of newly irrigated agricultural land in the province of Sind.[15] The local Sindhis naturally felt frustrated, and this was exploited fully by the Ayub governments. They diverted the bitterness towards the Partition refugees. The schism between the old Sindhis and new Sindhis widened.

Ayub's decision to shift the capital from Karachi to the suburbs of Rawalpindi on economic grounds was another blow to the Partition refugees. In February 1960, the new capital was named Islamabad. Ayub's decision to shift the capital was mainly with the motivation of keeping close contact with the General Headquarters of the Pakistan Army in Rawalpindi, but the rumour was that the site was close to his native village and it created new job opportunities for the people of the area. The commercial and industrial circles of Karachi were unhappy. The Muhajirs lost the convenient access to government offices they had enjoyed for a decade. For them, the job opportunities had also shrunk and their ability to influence the decision-making process was critically affected. The Ayub Government tried to pacify the Partition refugees by saying that Karachi had become too crowded because of the arrival of the refugees. Moreover, the government offices had grown in size during the previous ten years, and it was extremely expensive to build office space for the expanding government.[16] Such arguments, however, failed to quell the Muhajir disquiet. The post-Partition euphoria began to diminish and the tussle for power and favour began between local and non-local.

During the Ayub era, green revolution technologies were introduced in the agriculture sector. This resulted in mass exodus of peasants and small landowners, mostly from the Punjab. Many moved to Karachi. He also took aggressive initiatives to industrialize the country and much of the industrialization took place in Karachi. Karachi's share in large-scale industry went up to 28 per cent by

[14] Mehtab Ali Shah, *The Foreign Policy of Pakistan: Ethnic Impacts on Diplomacy 1971–1994*, London, New York: I.B. Tauris, 1997, p. 53.

[15] Burki, op. cit., n. 2 above, p. 37.

[16] Ibid., p. 35.

1954 and 44 per cent in 1964–5. This also attracted the uprooted peasants and others from Punjab and other provinces looking for jobs, shelter, and a new life.[17] This added a new element in the demographic complexities of Sind, and aroused concerns among the Partition refugees in Pakistan.

The discriminative policies of Ayub created a sense of alienation and deprivation among the Muhajirs. Intoxicated as they were by memories of their being the movers and shakers of the movement for Pakistan, the migrants had projected themselves as the new *messiahs*. These Partition refugees were further emboldened because of the fact that the city of Karachi was declared the capital city of the newly-created State of Pakistan. But the Ayubian policies put them off. They felt disowned, disempowered and cheated. The intelligentsia resented being governed by persons whom they considered intellectually far inferior; they were dismayed that the supreme power of the state was now being used against them; and they were convinced that Ayub's policies were against the refugees.

The presidential elections of 1964 added insult to injury. The opposition parties had put up Fatima Jinnah as their candidate. Miss Jinnah, sister of the founder of Pakistan, was widely respected for her contribution to the movement for Pakistan and for her integrity, honesty and love for Pakistan. She was pitted against Ayub Khan. Ayub won the elections through rigging, intimidation and high-handed measures. The voters were terrorized and bribed. Even then, Ayub had lost in Karachi and was barely tied with Miss Jinnah in Hyderabad. Ayub's son avenged himself on the Muhajirs by leading his father's victory procession in the Muhajir neighbourhood of Karachi and provoking clashes in which several persons were killed. The Muhajirs' enmity for Ayub Khan was sealed by the incident, and the seeds of hatred towards Pathans, who formed the larger part of the assaulting mob of Ayub's supporters, were sown.

[17] Syed Sikandar Mehdi, 'Migration, Multiculturalism and Integration: Developing Karachi as a Peace City', paper presented at a national seminar on the State of Migration and Multiculturalism in Pakistan, Islamabad, 16–18 June 2003.

In fact, the Partition refugees could never reconcile with the policies of Ayub and they came to the forefront in the rebellious movement against Ayub during 1969–71. Karachi became the epicentre of that movement. This was by far the most broad-based agitational movement that had arisen in the country. Although the undercurrent of Muhajir particularism had remained strong during this anti-Ayub agitation, the majority of the Muhajirs were not ready to accept ethnic separatism as a legitimizing principle in politics. They campaigned with the locals against the military dictator. Ayub couldn't control the movement, which had spread like wildfire in the length and breadth of the country. He resigned in March 1969, and General Yahya Khan took over the reins of power.

Within a few months of assuming power, Yahya Khan and his military colleagues dismantled the political system Ayub Khan had erected.[18] The early period of Yahya Khan's administration was reminiscent of Ayub's, with the publication of a stream of regulations designed to curb corruption and improve public discipline.[19] To facilitate return to parliamentary democracy, Yahya instituted a number of very significant changes in the political set-up.[20] Martial Law Regulation No. 58 established a system of accountability for civil servants, who could be dismissed for inefficiency, corruption, misconduct or subversive activities: 303 persons occupying high positions in the bureaucracy were dealt with under this regulation.[21] In its early stages, Yahya's regime kept the bureaucrats at arm's length from the decision-making process,[22] and general elections were held on 7 December 1970. These was the first transparent elections in the history of Pakistan. The Partition refugees generally cast their votes in favour of the Pakistan People's Party (PPP), a progressive, modernistic party under the leadership of a highly articulate, progressive, dynamic Sindhi

[18] Burki, op. cit., n. 2 above, p. 40.

[19] Ian Talbot, *Pakistan: A Modern History*, Lahore, Karachi, Islamabad: Vanguard Books, 1999 p. 190.

[20] Burki, op. cit., n. 2 above, p. 40.

[21] Talbot, op. cit., n. 19 above, p. 191.

[22] Ibid.

landlord, Zulfiqar Ali Bhutto, or for rightist or right-leaning parties including the Jamaat-i-Islami (JI), parties generally preferred by the military and conservative feudal lords. The Sindhis voted overwhelmingly for Bhutto.

During the period, large numbers of Pushtoons (Pathans) from NWFP looking for better opportunities migrated to the south and began competing with the blue-collar class in urban Sind.[23] These new migrants, through their hard work and contacts, came to dominate transport and building construction activities. They also acquired important positions in the police force in Karachi and were increasingly recruited as port and industrial labour.[24] Many Pushtoons opened hotels/restaurants to cater to Pushtoon labour, and others turned to transportation. A new class of Pushtoon settlers emerged in the rural parts of the province. Most of them were former army men. Factors like lack of economic opportunities in rural Punjab and Sind, growing concentration of industries and business in Karachi, and prospects for better wages there induced a scramble towards Sind, especially Karachi. This scramble from the Punjab and NWFP was officially encouraged. According to Arif Hasan, this migration towards the south was supported by the political patronage offered to them by the military rulers whose leaders also belonged to the NWFP.[25] The tremendous increase in Karachi's population from 2.044 million in 1961 to 3.606 million in 1971 was largely due to migration from other parts of Pakistan.[26]

In early 1970, Pakistan's military dictator General Yahya Khan took two major decisions. He restored the four original provinces in West Pakistan (including Sind) and accepted the Bengalis' overdue demand to restore the principle of one man, one vote.[27] The Bengalis were quite restive by then. Their major political party, the Awami League led by Sheikh Mujibur Rehman, had formulated a long list of grievances against the Central Government and West

[23] Malik, op. cit., n. 1 above, p. 201. In more recent times, 20,000 persons per annum have been settling in Karachi alone.

[24] Mehdi, op. cit., n. 17 above.

[25] Ibid.

[26] Ibid.

[27] Shah, op. cit., n. 14 above, p. 53.

Pakistani politicians. They demanded provincial autonomy and proclaimed a six-point programme. They also complained about their under-representation in the higher echelons of the military and bureaucracy and criticized the neglect of East Pakistan in the allocation of foreign aid, development funds and other resources. Sheikh Mujib also wanted to re-establish trade links and normal relations with India, which had remained suspended since the Indo-Pak war of 1965.[28] Elections were held on 7 December 1970. The PPP, under its charismatic leader Zulfiqar Ali Bhutto, won with a landslide victory in both Sind and Punjab,[29] and the Awami League emerged triumphant in East Pakistan. The Awami League obtained a clear-cut majority in the parliament. However, power was not transferred immediately to Sheikh Mujib. Bhutto flew to Dacca on 27 January 1971 for negotiations with Mujibur Rehman, but the Awami League leadership was not prepared to accept any amendment in the six-point formula, and the PPP leadership was not ready to concede all the six points.[30] Mujib wanted autonomy for East Pakistan, and Bhutto wanted restoration of civilian rule and restructuring of the economy and a place in the new government for PPP leaders. The Awami League insisted on its right to form the government and settle various issues through Parliament. Fearing that he wouldn't have a share in the new government and that the vital interests of the feudals and the military would be affected if the Awami league came to power, Yahya moved closer to Bhutto, and the situation in East Pakistan deteriorated. Soon after, Yahya announced postponement of the Parliament's session at Dhaka scheduled to be held on 3 March 1971.

The Awami League workers went on the rampage. Widespread arson and looting began in East Pakistan from the first week of March. The Awami League workers attacked and killed non-conformists and members of the Urdu-speaking community (refugees) and those who had moved to East Pakistan from West

[28] Rizvi, op. cit., n. 7 above, p. 179.

[29] Shah, op. cit., n. 14 above, p. 54.

[30] Z.A. Bhutto, *The Great Tragedy*, Karachi: People's Party, 1971, pp. 21–6.

Pakistan for business and trade. Their houses were burnt.[31] Yahya Khan launched Operation Searchlight against the Awami League. On 25 March, Mujib was arrested and taken to West Pakistan, and a number of his close associates escaped to Calcutta to form a government-in-exile. Soon, military resistance against West Pakistani forces began, and ultimately, the Pakistan Army was overwhelmed. It surrendered in a public ceremony on 16 December 1971.

The separation of East Pakistan affected the country critically. The Bengalis, who had constituted 56 per cent of Pakistan's population were no longer part of the ethnic equation. The Punjabis were now transformed into the new majority. Again, after thirteen years of military rule, the country was to be governed under a federal parliamentary system in which the voting strength was to depend on proportion of population in the new Pakistan, and the units of the federation were to be the four provinces. Thus, demography, status of immigrants and voting preference had destined the Muhajirs to have no effective representation in the national and Sind Governments. The creation of Bangladesh had serious implications for the Partition refugees. It, for example, seriously questioned the validity of the 'two nation theory', which had justified the creation of Pakistan and sustained the Muhajirs' faith in the state and in its future. If Islam could not hold the nation together, what else would? To many Muhajirs, the new, truncated Pakistan was only a shell of the original Pakistan premised on an ideological promise. Success of fissiparous tendencies in one region could be the harbinger of the rise of centrifugalism elsewhere. If the Sindhis succeeded as the Bengalis had, where would the Muhajirs go? Would they be treated like the outcast, persecuted Biharis in Bangladesh? The Muhajirs looked with great concern at the unfolding post-Yahya political scenario in Pakistan.

On 20 December 1971, Zulfiqar Ali Bhutto came to power and Yahya was deposed. His party was popular in former West Pakistan.[32] There were great expectations. Bhutto's political programme aimed at the total restructuring of Pakistan's economy.

[31] Ibid., p. 186.

[32] Shah, op. cit., n. 14 above, p. 54.

People were promised socialism: state control of the economy, and equal access by all people to such basic needs as food, health, education, and shelter.[33]

By 1973, the country had a new constitution and martial law was withdrawn. Further, the verdict of the Supreme Court of Pakistan passed unanimously in April 1972 declared that General Yahya Khan's assumption of power on 25 March 1969 was an act of 'usurpation' and was 'illegal and unconstitutional'.[34] It strengthened the civilian government further. This latest judgement was a reversal of the court's earlier judgement of 1958, which had legitimized Ayub's seizure of power by upholding a victorious revolution or a successful coup d'état as a recognized method of changing government.[35] The target of the new civilian leadership was a section of the Generals whose deep involvement in politics was criticized. In fact, the role of the Generals in Pakistani politics came under heavy fire during Bhutto's rule.

Furthermore, Bhutto was from Sind. In late December 1971, he became President of Pakistan. He was the first Sindhi to reach such a high position in the country and his cousin, Mumtaz Ali Bhutto, became the Chief Minister of Sind province. During Bhutto's era, the Sindhis, for the first time, enjoyed a degree of participation in the political process of the country, and, correspondingly, in its administration.[36] During the three decades after Independence, Sind was grossly neglected and it looked to Bhutto for redressal of the grievances. It wanted an end to its exploitation, a larger role for the locals in the decision-making process in the country, and a more assertive role for the natives in the province where the Partition refugees were still so powerful.

The migration of Indian Urdu-speaking Muslims to Sind had really affected the native Sindhis, a people who were progressively and systematically marginalized, deprived, and grossly neglected

[33] Burki, op. cit., n. 2 above, p. 42.

[34] See, *Asma Jilani vs. The Government of the Punjab and Others*, PLD, 1972, Supreme Court of Pakistan, pp. 139–270.

[35] Rizvi, op. cit., n. 7 above, p. 195.

[36] Shah, op. cit., n. 14 above, pp. 54–5.

during 1947–58 when the Partition refugees were occupying important political and governmental positions, and during 1958–71, when the Punjabi- and Pushtoon-dominated leadership reigned supreme.

As such, Bhutto's coming to power was welcomed enthusiastically as was Mumtaz Ali Bhutto's, and it was hoped that the grievances of local Sindhis would diminish. And, Mumtaz Bhutto did not disappoint them. The newly-elected provincial government of Mumtaz Bhutto moved a bill in the Sind Assembly in July 1972 for the promotion of Sindhi language, without prejudice to the status of the national language, Urdu.[37] The PPP Government wanted to restore the old status of Sindhi as the province's official language.[38] The move impressed both the staunch Sindhi nationalists and common Sindhi people. The time had come to rise for the protection of Sindhi cultural identity and teach the Urdu-speaking migrants a lesson. Feeling that they were being driven to the wall, the Partition refugees refused to accept anything less than a bilingual province.[39] They were not ready to let the special status be undermined by the Sindhi Government. They were living in big cities where native Sindhis were in minority. They came out on the streets and riots began over the language issue between the two communities of Sind.[40] Violent language riots between Sindhi and Partition refugees in the key urban areas were early signs of the seething hatred which was to grip the two linguistic groups in the 1980s. Sensing the gravity of the situation, Zulfiqar Bhutto intervened by issuing an ordinance. Superseding the Sindhi language act, it clearly stated that during the ensuing twelve years, no one eligible for employment in the provincial civil service was to be discriminated against simply on account of an inability to communicate in either Sindhi or Urdu. To assuage Muhajir grievances, the Chief Minister of Sind was changed: Mrs Liaquat Ali Khan, widow of the first Muhajir Prime Minister, was appointed

[37] Feroz Ahmed, *Ethnicity and Politics in Pakistan*, New York, Oxford, New Delhi: Oxford University Press, 1998, p. 41.

[38] Shah, op. cit., n. 14 above, p. 54.

[39] Ahmed, op. cit., n. 37 above, p. 41.

[40] Shah, op. cit., n. 14 above, p. 54.

Governor of Sind. A modern, multistoreyed market was built at a place burnt down during riots, and numerous other concessions were offered to the Partition refugees.[41] The PPP Government of Sind also tried to co-opt and pacify the Sindhi nationalists, moves which antagonized the Muhajirs in the process. Things were further complicated when Bhutto refused to bring back all the Indian migrants who had migrated to former East Pakistan after Partition, who generally supported West Pakistan and collaborated with the Pakistan military during the 1971 military operation. These were the Biharis, who wanted to go to Pakistan, wherever this was to be. But Bhutto did agree to bring some of these to the new Pakistan. A number of other important moves also helped the native Sindhis gain some confidence and encourage them to move to the urban areas of Sind—areas largely dominated by the Partition refugees. Bhutto tried to establish working relations with the urban Sindhis without alienating those in rural areas.[42] Again, he re-adopted a quota policy for recruitment to the central and provincial bureaucracies. This quota system was aimed at rectifying the under-representation of the Sindhis.[43] In Bhutto's regime, the Sindhis got many jobs in the nationalized sectors,[44] specially in the ministries of education and communication, headed by Sindhi ministers those days.[45]

During Bhutto's era, the steel mills became operational and a lot of job opportunities created. However, the competition for jobs intensified as the Partition refugees had to compete with the Punjabis, Pushtoons, and also with the Sindhis. They complained that the space created for the Sindhis in the steel mills, Pakistan International Airlines, federal and provincial bureaucracies, nationalized banks and other organizations was the space earlier

[41] Ayesha Jalal, *Democracy and Authoritarianism in South Asia: A Comparative and Historical Perspective*, Lahore: Sang-e-Meel Publications, 1995, p. 195.

[42] Malik, op. cit., n. 1 above, p. 187.

[43] Samina Ahmed, 'The Military and Ethnic Politics', in *Pakistan 1995–96*, ed. Charles H. Kennedy and Rasul Bakhsh Rais, Karachi, Lahore, Islamabad: Vanguard Books, 1995, p. 110.

[44] Singh, op. cit., n. 3 above, p. 517.

[45] Shah, op. cit., n. 14 above, p. 55.

occupied by Partition refugees. The alienation of the refugees increased further, and they felt that non-Urdu-speaking people, through quota preferences and ethnic nepotism, were superseding them. The quota system substantially diminished the Muhajirs' share in government services. Their influence in the upper echelons of the central bureaucracy was already marginalized because of the trend of Punjabi domination, which was accelerated by the ethnic restructuring of the services set in motion due to the separation of East Pakistan.[46]

Meanwhile, the Sindhis had their own grievances. They could not adjust to the separation of Karachi from the rest of Sind in 1948, and the one-unit scheme of 1955. The one unit scheme had especially imposed the domination of Punjab over other provinces, including Sind. It deprived Sind of whatever autonomy it had previously possessed, and also increased Muhajir control over Sind's affairs by virtue of their representation in the federal bureaucracy.[47] The educated Sindhis, who, in pre-Partition days, had dreamt of securing their due share of government jobs, were also disappointed. The separation of Karachi from Sind not only deprived Sind of considerable income, but was also seen by the Sindhis as an amputation of the head from the rest of the body. By and large, the Sindhis felt just like the American Indians in the USA they too were being persecuted on or in their own soil.[48]

As a result, conflict between local and non-local and over issues of ethnic identities became prominent in Pakistani politics. The conflict was not only between the Sindhis and Punjabis, but also between the old Sindhis and the new ones, the Partition refugees. The ethnic and political divide came to the fore, and in the countrywide movement against Bhutto's regime, a large member of alienated refugees took active part in the struggle for the removal of Bhutto. On 5 July 1977, Chief of the Army Staff, General Zia-ul-Haq removed Bhutto from power and took full control of the country. Bhutto was later sent to the gallows and Zia earned the

[46] Malik, op. cit., n. 1 above, p. 203.

[47] Ahmed, op. cit., n. 43 above, p. 109.

[48] Malik, op. cit., n. 1 above, p. 203.

distinction of becoming the longest-serving military ruler of the country. Subsequently, the country got polarized between those who supported and those who opposed Bhutto's PPP.[49]

However, Zia's military rule brought a sigh of relief to the Partition refugees, for it not only removed Bhutto and the Sindhi-majority provincial government from the scene, it also adopted a process of reversing the style and policies of the PPP, which had alienated the refugees. He also proclaimed on national television that the refugees deserved special favours because they had sacrificed everything for Pakistan.[50]

Zia imposed military rule over the country, and this continued until his death in August 1988. He declared that he considered the introduction of the Islamic system 'as an essential pre-requisite' for Pakistan.[51] Soon after, Bhutto's cultural policies were reversed and the airing of popular music of Pakistan's nationalities on radio and television was strictly banned. Instead, religious programmes and Islamic themes were stressed. Although the refugees did not enjoy this killjoy approach, the suppression of expression of cultural heterogeneity undoubtedly reduced their previous alarm and fostered a false sense of security.[52]

The strategies used by the Pakistani military rulers to stay in power included the manipulation of ethnic forces through divide and rule tactics, depoliticization of the society by weakening civil institutions, forging of alliances with anti-PPP political parties and anti-Bhutto groups by bribing them, dividing people on the *biradari* system in the Punjab, in particular, fomenting jihadi culture and fuelling sectarian violence.

Religious parties like the Jama'at-i-Islami (JI), Jamiat-ul-Ulema Pakistan (JUP) and the Anjuman-i-Sipah-e-Sahaba Party (ASSP) received official patronage from Zia's regime. They also filled their coffers with aid from countries like Saudi Arabia, Iraq, Libya and

[49] Mushahid Hussain, *Pakistan's Politics: The Zia Years*, Lahore: Progressive Publishers, 1990, p. 111.

[50] Ahmed, op. cit., n. 37 above, p. 117.

[51] Rizvi, op. cit., n. 7 above, p. 233.

[52] Ahmed, op. cit., n. 39 above, p. 118.

the Gulf States to help Zia implement his Islamization programme.[53] The state-sponsored process of Islamization dramatically increased sectarian divisions not only between Sunnis and Shias but also between Deobandis and Barelvis. The repercussions were grave for Karachi, a city of over a million people. The city was virtually sitting on an active volcano and the attention of people was diverted from the issues of military dictatorship, need for democratic governance, and the domination of Punjab over the rest of the country.

The ethnic domination of one ethnic group (the Punjabis) was now complete in Pakistan's politics. The important reality of Zia's period was that with the iron fist of military rule hidden inside an 'Islamic' glove, the government carried forward the Punjabization of power and privilege to its limit. Such an outcome was inherent in the hegemony of the military, which was and continues to be predominantly Punjabi.[54] As Pakistani scholar Muhammad Waseem (1988) puts it: 'With the imposition of martial law, the military personnel at all levels assumed responsible positions that enormously expanded Punjab's influence and prosperity.'[55] During Zia's regime, distribution of huge tracts of agricultural lands and urban residential plots took place on a large scale. In addition, commercial and industrial licences were given to retired military personnel on an unprecedented scale. The presence of the Punjabis in Karachi's bazaars, housing societies, colleges and universities was becoming more prominent. Muhajir youth faced difficulty in securing government jobs and Sindhi aspirations were nipped in the bud. Phenomenal growth of Punjabi power in Sind rekindled the old rivalry of the Muhajir middle class with its Punjabi counterparts. Similarly, hostility between the Pushtoons and the refugees also increased.

By this time, the Pushtoons had emerged as junior partners of the Punjabis in the military and bureaucracy. Punjabi and Pushtoon high civil and military officials assumed important positions in

[53] Shah, op. cit., n. 14 above, p. 138.
[54] Ahmed, op. cit., n. 39 above, p. 118.
[55] Shah, op. cit., n. 14 above, p. 51

government and semi-government departments and civil service positions in Sind. They also acquired important positions in the police and in government corporations. In the past, the Pushtoons had not been found able and could hardly compete with the Muhajirs for white-collar jobs or for admission to professional colleges. The Biharis arriving from Bangladesh, who had settled down in Karachi, found themselves competing with the Pushtoons for jobs in factories and for squatter settlements while the Partition refugees initially did not consider the Biharis as part of themselves and tension between the Pushtoons and Biharis didn't appear as a Muhajir problem, but when the Pushtoon–Bihari clashes began in the 1980s, the Pushtoons failed to distinguish between the old Muhajirs and the Biharis.

In the meantime, Afghan refugees began coming in waves, specially after December 1979, and many moved into Karachi via Baluchistan, NWFP and Punjab. From the early 1980s, a significant number of Afghan settlements sprouted in the city and its suburbs and nearly a million Afghans got settled. Many were attracted to the city for its better job prospects, business opportunities, educational facilities and access to the Gulf and the Middle East. The Afghan settlements mushroomed in the vicinity of the areas where the Pakistani Pushtoons were living. For them, the city was not a totally unfamiliar one in the sense that it already had a significant Pathan population from NWFP. By welcoming the Afghan refugees (Pushtoons), the Pushtoons of Karachi extended their glorious traditions of hospitality to the visitors. The Punjabi and Pushtoon population of Karachi, therefore, felt much more strengthened because of the arrival of the Afghans. Both reinforced each other and felt more secure.[56]

Zia's support for the Afghan resistance movement and his active involvement in the Afghan insurgency facilitated a dramatic increase in Pushtoon power in Karachi. The officially-tolerated Pushtoon smugglers market, called Bara Market at the head of the highway linking Karachi with Hyderabad, became a major national centre of the heroin trade, spurred by the Afghan war. The drug and gun

[56] Mehdi, op. cit., n. 17 above.

mafia, linked to the right-wing leadership of the Afghan rebels, also exercised control over Afghan refugees in Sind.[57]

The presence of over three million Afghan refugees on Pakistan soil sharpened the lines of social conflict by creating a parallel arms and drugs economy, widely believed to be linked with the army's notorious Inter-Services Intelligence (ISI).[58] The Muhajirs had probably lost their numerical majority in Karachi well before the separation of Bangladesh; they were further outnumbered because of the arriving Afghans. They did not benefit as much from the windfall of the Afghan war as did the Punjabi and Pushtoon community.

The city became even more unmanageable because of the growth of squatter colonies, frequent power failures, water scarcity, and breakdown of the municipal sanitation services, air pollution, chaotic traffic, road accidents, drug abuse, violence and crime. The new migrants were not only blamed for putting pressure on the city's meagre resources, the Pushtoons and Afghans were held directly responsible for pushing drugs, gunrunning, traffic fatalities and diverse criminal activities.[59]

Zia's regime was extremely centralized and unitary in character, and, therefore, the antithesis of the centrifugalism of the Sindhis. Thousands of Sindhis were purged from the public corporations and many lost their jobs with the denationalization of certain process units.[60] He deliberately adopted somewhat pro-Muhajir and anti-Sindhi policies and manipulated ethnic divisions in the province to weaken the political opposition.[61] The Sindhis were the main targets of military repression and their representation in the higher echelons of bureaucracy and military was reduced considerably.[62] Zia's regime also witnessed the creation and rise of the MQM, initially named the Muhajir Quami Movement

[57] Ahmed, op. cit., n. 39 above, p. 129.

[58] Jalal, op. cit., n. 41 above, p. 108.

[59] Ahmed, op. cit., n. 39 above, pp. 120–1.

[60] Ibid., p. 117.

[61] Ahmed, op. cit., n. 43 above, p. 112.

[62] Under Zia, there was no Sindhi above the rank of colonel in the army: ibid., p. 112.

(Refugee National Movement) and now known as the Muttahida Quami Movement (United Quami Movement), a party dominated by a middle-class and lower-middle-class Urdu-speaking Partition refugee leadership.

The emergence of Partition refugees as a powerful political force in urban Sind was welcomed by the establishment in Pakistan. It was, after all, going to sharpen the Sindhi–Muhajir divide and reduce the support bases of the PPP in urban Sind. By the 1980s, the MQM had already emerged as a powerful political force in urban Sind, but it was not to be allowed to gain enough power to upset the rules of the political game in Karachi, Sind and Pakistan and strike at the roots of the Punjabi–Pushtoon–dominated civil and military power in Sind and in the rest of Pakistan. It needed to be engaged mainly at the local/regional level.

In these circumstances, by the mid-1980s, the stage was set in Karachi for violence, and, accordingly, violent clashes took place between the old migrants (the migrants who came from India to Karachi and some other areas of urban Sind during and after 1947) and the new migrants—mainly Punjabis and Pushtoons—from other parts of Pakistan and the Afghan refugees. Subsequently, violent clashes took place between Partition refugees and Pathans, Punjabis and Afghans. Violent clashes also took place between newly-arriving Pakistanis from Bangladesh—the Biharis—and the Pushtoons of Pakistan and Afghanistan.[63] These clashes were exacerbated in 1985 when Bushra Zaidi, a Muhajir college girl, was run over and killed by a van being driven by a Pushtoon in a busy commercial area of a Muhajir-dominated section of Nazimabad. An angry mob tried to lynch the driver, while Pushtoons at first fought back the mob and then launched a premeditated armed attack on the Biharis living next to the Pushtoon settlements astride the industrial area in the western part of the city. Riots continued for several days during which scores of people were killed; curfew had to be imposed in the affected areas.

[63] Ibid.

These incidents not only intensified the hatred between the two groups, but also left the Muhajirs with a feeling that they had become powerless even in the streets of Karachi, a city supposed to be their secure habitat, and that the Government did not care for their plight.[64]

At this stage, the MQM appeared on the scene, and its leader Altaf Hussain spoke of the rights of Partition refugees. The MQM, formed in 1984, put forward a claim for the immigrants to be designated a fifth nationality in Pakistan.[65]

The emergence of the MQM in the mid-1980s, during the country's most oppressive and longest period of martial law, symbolized a shift of politics to the urban centres.

Since the mid-1980s, Sind, which is the second-biggest unit in the federation and formerly the most tranquil province, has been witnessing occasional spates of ethnic violence.[66] Riots between the descendants of Urdu-speaking refugees from India and the native Sindhi-speaking Sindhis in urban centres like Hyderabad and Karachi or riots between the settlers from other provinces with either of these two communities exacerbated by police brutalities have not only made headlines, but also proved to be the main challenge for the fragile post-Zia democracies.[67] Pakistan analysts have explained the eleven years of Zia's rule as the darkest phase of its history, which was marked by economic stagnation and loot of national wealth, pulverization of all opposition, and emasculation of all forms of dissent.[68] General Zia's Government (1977–88) planted conflicts in the length and breadth of the country and did not mind these conflicts blowing up into explosions, as these diverted the attention of the masses from his misgovernance and authoritarianism. He also promoted a jihadi culture and fuelled

[64] Ibid., p. 121.

[65] Shah, op. cit., n. 14 above, p. 57.

[66] Malik, op. cit., n. 1 above, p. 168.

[67] Ibid., p. 169. Ethnic volatility entered a critical phase in 1994–5 with daily occurrences of violence. The death figures just for the first six months of 1995 for Karachi stood at 1,000: based on the BBCWM Radio Report, monitored in Birmingham, UK, 11 July 1995.

[68] Singh, op. cit., n. 3 above, p. 518.

sectarian violence in Karachi and elsewhere.[69] Ethnic politics continued to play a nasty role. Armed groups proliferated in Pakistan, specially in urban Sind. There was easy access to arms and ethnic strife became increasingly explosive in the absence of political platforms and processes of give and take. Urban guerrillas, supported by the rank and file of their respective ethnic communities and financed by the landed cohorts and sometimes with support coming from across the borders, reduced life in Karachi and Hyderabad to a routine of arson, looting, street battles, sniper fire and prolonged curfews.[70]

However, the realization slowly dawned that the Partition refugees had to coexist with the Sindhis and members of other communities. After all, the Sindhis could not be wished away or perpetually marginalized. Further, the refugees had to come to terms with the Sindhi national aspirations if they wished to coexist with them. 'We don't want to become Biharis' was a popular slogan, expressing the desire not to be persecuted for having lived in perpetual hostility towards the host population. Likewise, the Sindhi nationalists realized that ethnic cleansing of the refugees was not possible, and confrontation between the two would weaken both. Again, the MQM was seeking legitimacy at the national level and struggling for more political space. As such, the MQM gradually revised, updated and upgraded its political agenda in order to force itself into the mainstream. But it was not easy. A study of the rise and struggle of the MQM may explain the point. It has been done in the next chapter.

[69] Mehdi, op. cit., n. 17 above.
[70] Malik, op. cit., n. 1 above, p. 169.

CHAPTER 4

Partition Refugees: Struggle for Empowerment and State's Response

On 11 June 1978, a student organization, the All Pakistan Muhajir Students Organization (All Pakistan Refugees Students Organization, APMSO) was established at Karachi University under the leadership of Altaf Hussain, a former student of Karachi University. The APMSO championed the cause of Partition refugees and raised demands of equal rights for the Indian migrants settled in Karachi and other areas of urban Sind. The organization instantly became popular among the Indian migrants (Partition refugees) and on 18 March 1984, it was converted into a full-fledged political party, named the Muhajir Quami Movement (Refugee National Movement, MQM).[1] The MQM proclaimed that the Muhajirs had had enough: they had to have a party of their own to fight for their rights, just as all other ethnic groups had parties to represent their interests.[2]

The word *muhajir* is derived from the Arabic *Hijra*, which was used to describe the migration of Prophet Muhammad (peace be upon him) and his followers from Mecca to Medina to avoid persecution by the enemies of Islam. Its later usage carried the connotation of a migration in the cause of Islam.[3] Muhajir is the

[1] Syed Sikandar Mehdi, 'Migration, Multiculturalism and Integration: Developing Karachi as a Peace City', paper presented at national seminars on the State of Migration and Multiculturalism in Pakistan, Islamabad, 16–18 June 2003.

[2] Feroz Ahmed, *Ethnicity and Politics in Pakistan*, Oxford, New York, New Delhi: Oxford University Press, 1998, p. 89.

[3] Ibid., p. 91.

term which was used by the Muslims who migrated from India to Pakistan at the time of Partition. A little more than 70 per cent of these refugees in (West) Pakistan were Punjabis, who settled mainly in Pakistani Punjab,[4] spoke the same language, and shared the same culture. They assimilated rather quickly with the indigenous population in West Punjab. However, the one million Urdu-speaking refugees who came from the United Provinces or UP (now Uttar Pradesh), Central Province or CP (now Madhya Pradesh), Ajmer and Rajputana (now Rajasthan), Hyderabad (now Andhra Pradesh), and Bihar settled mostly in Sind, and continued to maintain the Muhajir label for group identification. Their large and compact settlement in an urban environment allowed for the formation of a cultural identity well protected from local influence. Following the traditions of Islamic Hijra, these immigrants insisted on being called 'Muhajirs'.[5] The MQM provided a political identity to them and attained instant popularity.

The immigrants had held important positions in the new country and wielded enormous influence in business, much greater than their proportion in the national population. But when the people from other provinces, initially Punjabis and then Pushtoons, began to outbid the Muhajirs, the latter felt uneasy.[6] They felt that, despite their role in the making of Pakistan and their high literacy rate, they were being superseded by non-Urdu-speakers. Besides this, they often complained that they were ill-treated by non-Muhajirs, who relished ridiculing Urdu-speakers by taunting them as timid imbeciles. The local people began describing or lumping them as 'Hindustani' (Indians) or *panahguzeen* (those who have sought refuge; asylum seekers). The most interesting and astonishing thing was that the second generation of Partition refugees born in Sind were also ill-treated and pushed to describe

[4] Feroz Ahmed, 'Ethnicity, State and National Integration', *Pakistan Perspectives*, vol. 4, no. 2, July–December 1999, p. 27. See *Census of Pakistan 1951*, vol. I, General Report and Tables for Pakistan, Karachi: Government of Pakistan, 1951.

[5] Ahmed, op. cit., n. 2 above, p. 92.

[6] Iftikhar H. Malik, *State and Civil Society in Pakistan Politics of Authority, Ideology and Ethnicity*, New York, London: St. Martin's Press and Macmillan, 1997, p. 231.

itself as refugees. The MQM, in later years, made them feel proud as Muhajirs or refugees.

But meanwhile, an acceleration of Punjabi migration had taken place. There was, in addition, an increasing Punjabi role in the expanding bureaucracy at the expense of the Muhajirs.[7] Simultaneously, the Pushtoons increased their stranglehold on the city's transport, labour market and construction industries.[8] The Sindhi language controversy in 1972, the new quota system for federal employment, and ethnicization of politics in the 'partyless' elections in a Punjabi-dominated state disturbed the Indian refugees in Sind.[9] They found themselves squeezed out of employment and were angered by the ostentatious display of new money, which accompanied the flood of guns and heroin from the areas adjacent to the Afghan war zone.[10]

Altaf Hussain put these dreads, suspicions and fears together and offered a new strategy for dealing with the challenge. Eventually, the MQM was created at Karachi.

Indeed, Karachi and the MQM have remained intertwined—like Hussain and the MQM. The enigmatic personality of Altaf Hussain has left a deep imprint on the MQM. Son of Nazir Hussain, a railway employee with limited economic means, Altaf Hussain was born in Karachi on 17 September 1953. He underwent military training for a year in the National Cadet Corps, a college-based training programme for civilian youth in Pakistan. It was here that Hussain developed certain attitudes. He was not happy with the way he was treated by the non-Muhajir cadets and non-Muhajir students at Karachi University when he commenced his postgraduate career in the Pharmacy Department. Hussain deeply

[7] See Feroz Ahmed, 'Ethnicity and Politics: The Rise of Muhajir Separatism', *South Asia*, vol. VIII, nos. 1, 2, Spring 1988, p. 50, referred to in Ian Talbot, *Pakistan: A Modern History*, Lahore, Karachi, Islamabad: Vanguard Books, 1999, p. 265.

[8] Ibid., p. 265.

[9] Ian Talbot, 'Back to the Future? Pakistan, History, and Nation Building', in *Pakistan at the Millennium*, ed. Charles H. Kennedy, Kathleen McNiel, Carl Ernst and David Gilmartin, Karachi: Oxford University Press, 2003, pp. 73–4.

[10] Talbot, op. cit., n. 7 above, p. 265.

resented ethnic jokes about Muhajirs and was assaulted by activists of a dominant student party, the Islami Jamiat-i-Tulaba (IJT). The IJT's tough tactics were instrumental in alienating a number of Urdu-speaking students in the 1980s in Karachi University. The fragmentation of mainstream politics in the country during martial law and the stigmatization of Urdu-speakers by other ethnic groups on campuses gave birth to a new sense of Muhajir identity.[11]

The APMSO was established in reaction to the unilateral policies of the IJT at Karachi University. Hussain was one of the founding members of the APMSO at this university. He started working with other leaders like Azeem Tariq, Aamir Khan, Farooq Sattar, Abdul Razzak, Aafaq Ahmed, Imran Farooq and others. The APMSO successfully challenged the hold of the IJT and other ethnic, regional and ideological bodies over the students' union and the marginalization of the IJT and other student groups began. Enjoying its new-found glory, the APMSO began to relish its supremacy on the campuses and in the colleges in Karachi.[12]

After experiencing a leadership role in student politics, Hussain went to the US and worked as a taxi driver in Chicago. The city of Al Capone and its tough neighbourhoods hardened him. In his leisure time, he read books on political philosophy, leadership, and people's movements.[13] On his return to Karachi, he institutionalized his ideas and schemes into the rubric of the movement and decided to expand its activism. He cast himself in the role of a leader.[14]

Hussain built an extensive network with strong roots in the Muhajir-dominated areas of Karachi like Azizabad, Orangi town, Baldia, Korangi, Nazimabad and other urban localities and streets of Muhajir settlement. Young volunteers who came in the hundreds were catapulted into leadership roles in the most important city, and Hussain's rhetoric, ambiguous demagogy and forceful gestures attracted the youthful Muhajirs immensely.

[11] Malik, op. cit., n. 6 above, p. 231.

[12] Ibid., p. 232.

[13] Younis Ahmed, 'The Rise and fall of Altaf Hussain', *Herald*, October 1998, pp. 62–4.

[14] Malik, op. cit., n. 6 above, p. 232.

Altaf Hussain soon emerged as chief spokesman of the Partition refugees. On 14 August 1979, while leading a procession to the tomb of the Quaid-i-Azam in Karachi, he was arrested by martial law authorities who sentenced him to a year in prison in addition to many lashes. After his release, he became an even stronger advocate of Urdu-speakers in Sind.[15] On 18 June 1984, the MQM was formally launched. The party was welcomed by Partition refugees and offered hope to a people viewing themselves as the most deprived and oppressed group in Pakistan.[16]

The MQM spread like a whirlwind throughout the city and continued with strong organizational work in Hyderabad and Sukkur, though Karachi remained the major arena of its activities, including inter-factional rivalry for the control of powerful, diverse Muhajir constituencies.[17] The emergence of the MQM in the mid-1980s, during the country's most oppressive and longest period of martial law, symbolized a shift of politics to urban centres and accentuated inter-ethnic tension.[18] Under Hussain's leadership, the MQM emerged as a well-organized party with a trained and armed body of supporters, who were frequently deployed against ethnic rivals. The resultant increase in ethnic hostilities was used in turn to strengthen and expand the MQM's base of support.[19]

The MQM is an exceptional movement in the recent history of Pakistan. It has certain specific characteristics. It is predominantly urban and class-specific. Its youthful membership is mobilized in the name of ethnicity and motivated by radical ideas.[20] It is a party of youth which reflects current demographic realities in Pakistan. All its leaders at the time of its formation were in their twenties. It included unemployed youth, the educated unemployed

[15] Ibid., p. 231.

[16] Ahmed, op. cit., n. 4 above, p. 55. For an analysis of the rise of the Muhajir movement, see Feroz Ahmed, 'Ethnicity and Politics: The Rise of Muhajir Separatism', *South Asia*, vol. VIII, nos. 1 and 2, Spring 1988, pp. 33–45.

[17] Malik, op. cit., n. 6 above, p. 234.

[18] Ibid., p. 203.

[19] Samina Ahmed, 'The Military and Ethnic Politics' in *Pakistan 1995–96*, ed. Charles H. Kennedy and Rasul Bakhsh Rais, Karachi, Lahore, Islamabad: Vanguard Books, 1995, p. 114.

[20] Malik, op. cit., n. 6 above, p. 223.

and underemployed, and evolved from the student cadres of Karachi University. In addition and equally significantly, the MQM has had the largest proportion of educated membership of all the national parties except the JI. The MQM received steady support from its financiers, of whom there was no scarcity, and helping hands from various walks of life in Karachi, and, subsequently Hyderabad, Nawabshah, and Sukkur.

The MQM has the largest urban representation among all political parties. It is a party of the middle classes and the poor. Its founders and most of its activists represent the lower-middle class who had suffered unemployment and abuse of power by the police, bureaucracy and the feudal classes. The movement was aware of its power-base in terms of demographic realities and virtually created an ethnic identity from what had been merely a fleeting ideal to members of the previous generation. Its networking, unending supply of volunteers, funds and mobility helped it create a Muhajir identity.

Hussain emerged as the most powerful and charismatic leader and commanded the organization from 90 Azizabad, which worked as the headquarters, and where dignitaries including prime ministers and governors were received. He assumed uncontested leadership by means of dedication, rhetoric, demagogy, ambiguity, and coercion. For a long time, he remained the focal point through a combination of charisma, propaganda, machination and the highly disciplined structure of the movement. He was made into a cult figure (*pir*) and opposition to him was often forcefully silenced, and myths were woven around his supreme authority and personality. He assumed the position of a godfather for the Muhajirs.[21]

The MQM entered the political arena at a point when the Muhajirs seriously felt the need for such an organization and had begun to accept the legitimacy of its proclaimed ethnic-specific articulation of their interests. It profited enormously from the ethnic clashes of the 1980s and helped in the crystallization of Muhajir nationalism by becoming the sole authentic representative of the

[21] Ibid., pp. 224–33.

Muhajir view of the dispute.[22] It put forward a claim for the migrants to be designated as a fifth nationality.[23] It rose to prominence at a time in Pakistan when political processes was held in abeyance by a military regime which deemed the articulation of sectional interests to be less dangerous than the growth of a nationally-based political party.[24]

The themes of Muhajir unity, sacrifice and victimization came out strongly in the flood of literature produced by the MQM. The following introductory paragraph taken from a pamphlet entitled *Background of the Muhajir Nation and a Brief History of MQM*, encapsulates the Muhajir historical discourse:

> The Muhajirs, distinguished from others in Pakistan by their distinct culture and civilization, language, aesthetic and artistic aspiration, had immigrated to Pakistan from undivided India in 1947 and thereafter, as a matter of right of undivided India felt threatened to live with honour and dignity under the Hindus and, therefore, struggled for the creation of a promised land, Pakistan. The pseudo-politicians and people of present Pakistan opposed its creation until it became imminent. Pakistan was created on the basis of [the] two-nation theory, a separate state for the Muslims. Pakistan was created for the entire Muslims of undivided India and not only for the Muslims of the present Pakistan and former East Pakistan (now Bangladesh) . . . soon after the creation of Pakistan, Muhajirs faced systematic and persistent discrimination and prejudice from the indigenous feudo-politicians . . . afraid of the immigrants playing a vital role in the development of the country.[25]

In the light of the above-mentioned statement, the MQM defined Muhajirs as the fifth nationality in Pakistan[26] and championed the interests of the Urdu-speaking Partition refugees. Rather than focusing its attention on military dictatorship or democratic rights of the Pakistani people, the MQM focused

[22] Ahmed, op. cit., n. 2 above, pp. 124–5.

[23] Mehtab Ali Shah, *The Foreign Policy of Pakistan: Ethnic Impacts on Diplomacy 1971–1994*, London, New York: I.B. Tauris, 1997, p. 57.

[24] Ayesha Jalal, *Democracy and Authoritarianism in South Asia: A Comparative and Historical Perspective*, Lahore: Sang-e-Meel Publications, 1995, p. 196.

[25] Talbot, op. cit., pp. 74–5.

[26] Malik, op. cit., n. 6 above, p. 225.

exclusively on the demands of one particular ethnic community[27] and urged the cessation of *zulm* perpetrated on the Muhajir *quam* and repatriation of stranded Pakistanis from Bangladesh.[28] Later, the leaders of the MQM, who demanded the recognition of Muhajirs as a separate nationality,[29] claimed to represent the people of other linguistic groups as well.[30] In other words, they insisted on a broader definition of the term *muhajir* that included not only the Urdu-speaking people who had migrated from India, but also all other non-Punjabi groups whose members also migrated from India and settled in Sind, such as Hyderabadis, Gujaratis, Madrasis, Kutchi Memons, Khojas from Bombay, Ghanchis, and more recently Biharis, Bengalis, and some others.

The Muhajirs' quest for identity eventually found expression in the MQM's thesis of Muhajirs as Pakistan's fifth nationality. Initially, implicit in the idea was the demand for a separate space for this nationality: partition of Sind to create a Muhajir province.[31] At different times, the demand for a separation of urban areas from rural Sind or division of Sind and designation of urban Sind as Muhajir *subah* or its internationalization as a new Hong Kong has been put forward by the MQM.

According to its manifesto, the MQM is a progressive organization in favour of land reforms, an end to the quota system, the preservation of cultural heritage, lowering of the age of voting from 21 to 18, reorganization of constituencies, and other electoral reforms. It also favoured the decentralization of central and provincial powers by redistributing them among the elected local councillors. In its manifestos and other policy statements, it promised an egalitarian taxation system, equal opportunities in education, and reorganization of the transport system in urban

[27] Ahmed, op. cit., n. 2 above, p. 89.

[28] Malik, op. cit., n. 6 above, p. 225.

[29] Ahmed, op. cit., n. 4 above, p. 34. The 25-point Charter of Resolutions in 1988 stated: 'Muhajirs Should be Constitutionally Declared a Separate Nationality in Pakistan': reprinted in *News*, 14 October 1994.

[30] Shah, op. cit., n. 23 above, p. 57.

[31] Iqbal Akhund, *Trial-Error: The Advent and Eclipse of Benazir Bhutto*, Karachi: Oxford University Press, 2000, pp. 286–7.

Sind.[32] With a youthful spirit endowed with unlimited energy and manpower, these student leaders, many of whom had acquired experience of militancy from the IJT, began challenging urban issues like the quota system, unemployment, and emigration from up-country.[33]

The rise of the MQM has been accompanied by an unprecedented media campaign by the party and intellectuals supporting its ideology and positions. As a result, many social issues interfacing with the ethnic question have come into sharp focus. Simultaneously, many myths have also been propagated, which tend to muddy the political waters and make the resolution of the problem even more difficult.[34]

The partyless elections of 1985 further encouraged ethnic and *biradari* loyalties. The political responses to this situation were seen in the Muhajirs' claims that they should be recognized as a fifth nationality,[35] and in the formation of Punjabi–Pushtoon *ittehad* in March 1987.[36]

The MQM was very much a product of socio-economic changes of the Zia era in Karachi.[37] In September 1986, a protest march organized by the MQM in Karachi near Sohrab Goth was stopped by the police in typical brutal South Asian manner, which resulted in the movement gaining more popularity among the Muhajirs of urban Sind irrespective of their age, sex or geographic background. In December 1986, the Chief Minister had ordered the launch of the slum clearance operation at Sohrab Goth by the army and police against the dens of the drug mafia with a heavy Pushtoon and Afghan concentration. In retaliation, they turned the tables on

[32] Malik, op. cit., n. 6 above, p. 224.

[33] Ibid., p. 231. For a detailed analysis, see Anwar A. Syed, 'Political Parties and the Nationality Question in Pakistan', *Journal of South Asian and Middle Eastern Studies*, vol. XII, no. I, Fall 1988, pp. 42–75.

[34] Ahmed, op. cit., n. 2 above, p. 136.

[35] Talbot, op. cit., n. 9 above, p. 265. Muhajirs had previously always identified with Pakistani Islam rather than with the community: this was demonstrated in their traditional support for the JI.

[36] Talbot, op. cit., n. 7 above, p. 265.

[37] Ibid., p. 265.

the Muhajirs in the neighbourhood and well-armed gangs from the Goth invaded Muhajir colonies and mayhem ensued. This proved to be a turning point in inter-ethnic relations in Karachi, leading to indiscriminate killings, riots and curfews.[38] Karachi experienced communal carnage of a magnitude that Pakistan had not witnessed since the bloodbath that accompanied the Partition of India in 1947.[39] The MQM, however, disclaimed any role in the riots.[40]

Articulating Muhajir demands such as increased representation in the quota for civil service employment, the MQM won local body polls in Karachi and Hyderabad in 1987[41] through its organizational acumen and youthful energy.[42] The ethnic riots in urban Sind during 1986 and 1987 helped to mobilize the Muhajirs and expand the MQM's support base, specially among students and unemployed or underemployed youth.[43] The easy availability of weapons due to the Afghan war and the pressure of Afghan refugees in Karachi drove the MQM to prepare itself for all kinds of challenges. It is alleged that it also received encouragement from intelligence agencies, which were trying to curtail the influence of the PPP.[44] The 1987 local government non-party municipal elections in Karachi and Hyderabad impacted on its relations with the Sindhi community. In rural Sind, the MQM confronted the hostile Sindhi population and during the 1980s, riots erupted between Muhajirs and Sindhis. By 1987, ethnic violence became endemic in Sind, forcing the civil administration to rely on direct army assistance on several occasions.[45]

Since its inception the MQM had to face the hostility of various groups, political forces, military intelligence as well as different governments, though many allege that the MQM enjoyed official patronage during the Zia regime through state intelligence

[38] Malik, op. cit., n. 6 above, p. 236.

[39] Ahmed, op. cit., n. 2 above, p. 90.

[40] Ibid., p. 90.

[41] Ahmed, op. cit., n. 19 above, p. 113.

[42] Malik, op. cit., n. 6 above, p. 237.

[43] Ahmed, op. cit., n. 19 above, pp. 113–14.

[44] Malik, op. cit., n. 6 above, p. 232.

[45] Ahmed, op. cit., n. 19 above, p. 114.

agencies.[46] A number of writers even claim that the ISI sponsored the MQM to weaken the PPP and the Movement for the Restoration of Democracy (MRD) in Sind. Altaf Hussain, who soon emerged as the dominant figure in the MQM, has always denied these charges.[47]

Zia's death in August 1988 was followed by a transfer of power to civilian hands after the general elections held in November 1988 on party basis. The PPP obtained a majority in rural Sind in the elections of 1988; the MQM captured most of the seats in urban Sind.[48]

Although the PPP was deprived of an absolute majority at the centre, it still emerged as the largest party in the National Assembly and managed to muster a slim majority with the support of smaller parties and independents. It was also in a position to set up governments in Sind and the NWFP by forging electoral alliances.[49]

After the victory of the PPP in rural areas and the MQM in the urban parts of the province, the two parties moved closer and signed a 58-point agreement in December 1988.[50] The prospects looked good when the PPP reached an accord with the MQM before coming to power in 1988. The PPP had, since the time of the Zulfiquar Ali Bhutto, managed to stem Sindhi extremism, and now, under Benazir, it had trounced the Sindhi nationalist parties in the elections.[51]

However, before the PPP could form the Government at the Centre, the military wanted to create a credible civilian alliance to act as a counterweight to the strongest political party, the PPP. It is generally believed that the ISI helped the formation of a coalition of nine right-wing pro-Islamic and anti-PPP parties, the Islami Jamhouri Ittehad (IJI). After elections, the PPP had to agree to the continuation of the army's defence and foreign policies, accept the military's internal autonomy, and retain Ghulam Ishaq Khan

[46] Malik, op. cit., n. 6 above, p. 231.

[47] Ibid., p. 229. See also Talbot, op. cit., n. 9 above, pp. 264–5.

[48] Jalal, op. cit., p. 196.

[49] Ahmed, op. cit., n. 19 above, p. 115.

[50] Malik, op. cit., n. 6 above, p. 238.

[51] Akhund, op. cit., n. 31 above, p. 228.

as President until the end of his five-year term.[52] In the context of Sindhi politics, the absence of a clear majority in the National Assembly and the presence of a strong and hostile IJI opposition forced the PPP to rely on the MQM to retain its hold over the Centre,[53] and rule over Sind with ease.

In 1988, Benazir Bhutto formed a coalition government with the MQM in both Sind and at the Centre.[54] At the same time, the Sindhi nationalists, outvoted by the PPP and the MQM, entered a period of cynical chauvinism with attacks on both parties. The mutual interdependence of the PPP and the MQM due to their electoral and logistic needs did not allow any major crack in the first ten months of Bhutto's regime.[55] But this marriage of convenience did not last long.[56] The agreement had a troubled existence during its brief life. Friction between the partners began almost at once over small matters. When Benazir came to Karachi after being sworn in as Prime Minister, the MQM chief, Altaf Hussain, did not pay a courtesy call, citing sickness as the cause, and sent a delegation under a deputy. The MQM delegation was kept waiting because of her meeting with the envoy of Rajiv Gandhi, the Indian leader which went on longer than expected.[57] The cracks began to grow. Hussain had successfully pressurized Benazir Bhutto to accept a number of Muhajir demands in the December 1988 Karachi Accord. It included the repatriation of 250,000 stranded Pakistanis—commonly known as 'Biharis'—from Bangladesh and replacement of the distinction between urban and rural Sind in the bureaucracy's employment quotas by Sindhi and Muhajir categories.[58] A more serious problem arose when Benazir

[52] Ahmed, op. cit., n. 19 above, p. 115. For details, see Hassan Askari Rizvi, *The Military and Politics in Pakistan*, Lahore: Progressive Publishers, 1986, pp. 38–9.

[53] Ibid.

[54] Shah, op. cit., n. 23 above, p. 59.

[55] Malik, op. cit., n. 6 above, p. 238.

[56] Shah, op. cit., n. 23 above, p. 59.

[57] Akhund, op. cit., n. 31 above, p. 288.

[58] Ahmed, op. cit., n. 19 above, p. 116.

Bhutto withdrew the permission she had given for a small number of Biharis to come to Pakistan.[59]

The PPP thought that it was in no position to implement these demands without eroding its Sindhi support base, while the Karachi Accord provided Sindhi nationalist parties such as Jiye Sindh and the Sindh National Front (SNF) a pretext to attack the government.[60] The two parties were divided by a basic incompatibility of approach and philosophy. The PPP has an ethnic base in Sind, but remains an all-Pakistan party with countrywide roots and a national agenda.[61] For a variety of reasons, it refused to respect the provisions of the Karachi Accord.

The MQM accused the PPP of having reneged on some points in the Karachi Accord and held the extremists in the PPP responsible for the breakdown. The accusation may be true to some extent, for the feudal rivals of Sind Chief Minister, Qaim Ali Shah left no stone unturned to dislodge him.[62]

Moreover, the non-implementation of the accord and the extension of patronage to the PPP's Sindhi constituents through, for example, preferential employment policies, led to tension between the MQM and the Bhutto Government.[63]

The PPP and the MQM failed to forge a *modus vivendi* in Sind and a reign of anarchy descended on the rural and urban areas of the province. Dacoities and kidnappings became the order of the day.[64] The MQM reacted violently. An antagonized MQM reverted to its *modus operandi*. Use of violence for ethnic mobilization and for the attainment of political goals[65] became the order of the day and armed bands became active, sniping, looting, and kidnapping in Karachi and the rest of Sind. The MQM and PPP faced each other with mistrust, hatred and vengeance in Karachi and the rest

[59] Akhund, op. cit., n. 31 above, pp. 288–9.

[60] Zahid Hussain, 'Sindh: A Province Held to Ransom', *Newsline*, August 1989, p. 18.

[61] Akhund, op. cit., n. 31 above, p. 289.

[62] Ahmed, op. cit., n. 2 above, pp. 127–8.

[63] Ahmed, op. cit., n. 19 above, p. 116.

[64] Jalal, op. cit., n. 24 above, p. 196.

[65] Ahmed, op. cit., n. 19 above, p. 116.

of Sind. Not much later, hostilities broke out between activists of the two parties, which reversed the trend of rapprochement between them.

Relations deteriorated to such an extent that on 18 September 1989, the MQM formally joined hands with the Combined Opposition Parties (COP) in co-sponsoring a no-confidence motion against Prime Minister Benazir Bhutto. The COP rally on the grounds of the Quaid-i-Azam mausoleum at Karachi on 26 January 1990 was a personal triumph for Altaf Hussain. It displayed to the full the MQM leader's charisma and oratorial skills. This was undoubtedly the largest political gathering in Pakistan's history.

In February 1990, when the Pakistanis supported Bhutto overwhelmingly on her stance over the Kashmir crisis and the international media reported imminent hostilities between India and Pakistan, the MQM called for a strike, which turned into a bloody affair. The confrontation between the administration and MQM protesters led to many casualties. During this spate of ethnic violence, both sides reportedly carried out organized kidnapping, sniping and lynching in secret torture cells.[66]

This strike left 60 dead and 100 injured in Karachi. Earlier, activists of the Sindh National Alliance (SNA) demanding the creation of an independent Sindhu Desh had occupied the Sukkur airport and burnt the Pakistani flag. In Hyderabad, Sindhi policemen refused to fire on fellow Sindhis. Two Muhajir brothers, both members of the PPP, were kidnapped and shot dead at their parents' doorstep in Karachi. Their killer was reportedly let out on bail by a sympathetic magistrate.[67]

In protest at the killing of the Muhajirs, Hussain began a hunger-strike on Sunday, 8 April 1990. The following Thursday, a panel of doctors examined him for an hour and came to the conclusion that his life was in danger.[68] It was only after an appeal by a number of COP leaders who had come to Karachi that he broke his fast. He was being treated for kidney problems at the Princess

[66] Malik, op. cit., n. 6 above, p. 242.

[67] Akhund, op. cit., n. 31 above, p. 283.

[68] Talbot, op. cit., n. 7 above, p. 307.

Grace Hospital in London when the tide of violence reached its peak.[69] The MQM gave frequent calls for strike in Karachi, which paralysed the provincial machinery.[70]

Despite a continuing depressing round of curfews and killings in Karachi, the crisis in Sind came to a climax in Hyderabad with the Pucca Qila incident of 27 May 1990.[71] In an attempt to reassert its authority over Sind, the PPP conducted a hastily-planned and badly-implemented operation against MQM activists in Hyderabad.[72] This episode, which has been likened by the Muhajir leaders to the Jallianwala Bagh massacre,[73] remains shrouded in controversy.

The Pucca Qila area in the centre of Hyderabad is a Muhajir locality, and on the day of the massacre, a Sindhi police party entered[74] and looked for militants hiding near Pucca Qila. It recovered suspected illegal arms and the police clashed with predominantly Muhajir groups. This resulted in a massive number of casualties.[75] The police opened fire, allegedly killing over 40 people and wounding many more, while the police version of events explained the firing as retaliation to sniping. The MQM maintained that it was indiscriminate. Many of the victims were women and children. The MQM said that the women were carrying copies of the Koran over their heads and pleading for the police to stop the massacre.[76] The next day, snipers retaliated in Karachi.[77] A busload of workers going home from work was stopped and its 21 passengers shot dead.[78]

[69] Ibid.

[70] Ahmed, op. cit., n. 19 above, p. 117.

[71] Talbot, op. cit., n. 7 above, p. 307.

[72] Ahmed, op. cit., n. 19 above, p. 117.

[73] Talbot, op. cit., n. 7 above, p. 307. For example, Secretary-General of the MQM, Dr Imran Farooq declared on 23 August 1990: 'The Pucca Qila firing in Hyderabad has superseded the Jallianwala Bagh, Amritsar tragedy and Ms. Benazir Bhutto has gone one step ahead of General Dyer': *Daily Dawn*, 24 Aug. 1990.

[74] Ibid.

[75] Malik, op. cit., n. 6 above, p. 242.

[76] Talbot, op. cit., n. 7 above, p. 307.

[77] Malik, op. cit., n. 6 above, p. 242.

[78] Akhund, op. cit., n. 31 above, p. 283.

The Army was called in to patrol the streets and localities under curfew. The induction of the army for law and order on a large scale raised a number of serious questions, including the vulnerability of the political system itself.[79] Emotional appeals from certain groups and individuals were made to the army for a formal takeover, though the Generals stated that they were not interested in imposing martial law in Sind during such times.[80]

The ethnic fragility in Sind continued throughout the eighteen months of Benazir Bhutto's Government, often in the face of daily incidents of kidnapping for ransom and dacoities in urban areas. Issues such as repatriation of the Biharis from Bangladesh or emigration from Punjab and NWFP to Sind continued to fan ethnic discontent.[81] By the mid-1990s, the Muhajir audiences were chanting *'Sind mein hoga kaise guzara: adha hamara adha tumhara'* (How can we coexist in Sind: half is ours, half yours).[82] In the tense circumstances, the MQM decided to break its coalition, and, finally, in June 1990, the MQM's partnership with the PPP Government was broken.

The Urdu-speaking head of the Pakistan Army, General Aslam Beg, began issuing statements against Benazir's Government for its failure to accommodate the MQM's interests.[83] General Beg was reportedly also resentful because Benazir wanted to promote General Alam Jan Mahsood with the intention of appointing him Chief of the Army Staff after Beg's anticipated retirement in 1991. Benazir's Government was finally dismissed both at the Centre and in Sind on 6 August 1990.

After the dissolution of the PPP Government on 6 August 1990 through a presidential proclamation alleging corruption, nepotism and widespread lawlessness,[84] a caretaker government was set up. The leader of the new government was a feudal Sindhi,

[79] Malik, op. cit., n. 6 above, p. 242.
[80] Ibid., p. 243.
[81] Ibid., p. 240.
[82] Talbot, op. cit., n. 7 above, p. 266.
[83] Shah, op. cit., n. 23 above, p. 59.
[84] Malik, op. cit., n. 6 above, p. 244.

Ghulam Mustafa Jatoi.[85] He acted as interim Prime Minister until Nawaz Sharif could take over as Pakistan's next Prime Minister.[86] This shadow military government was then given the task of overseeing the holding of general elections in October 1990. In the run-up to the elections and during the polling itself, the interim government extended its complete support to Nawaz Sharif's IJI. The president and the ISI reportedly helped to formulate a joint IJI electoral strategy against the PPP, and IJI candidates were actively assisted by the central and provincial administrations.[87] As a reward for Ghulam Mustafa Jatoi's role in rigging elections in Sind, Jam Sadiq (a PPP dissident) was appointed caretaker Chief Minister[88] of Sind and given the task of containing the PPP.[89] Jam Sadiq carried out his responsibilities by forging alliances with the MQM, the Muslim League, Sindhi nationalists, and some PPP dissidents.[90] The Jam Sadiq administration moved against the PPP by arresting its electoral candidates and polling agents and intimidating its supporters. At the same time, a military-sponsored deal was struck between the MQM and the IJI, as the MQM extended its support to the interim government at the Centre and in Sind.[91] In the next few months, Jam Sadiq's harsh actions against PPP activists in Sind kept both Islamabad and Azizabad (the MQM head office) happy.[92]

The IJI alliance won a clear majority in the National Assembly elections, enabling Nawaz Sharif to form a government with a two-third's majority at the Centre.[93] The formation of the Nawaz Sharif Government at the Centre as well as in all the four provinces

[85] Ahmed, op. cit., n. 19 above, p. 118.

[86] Shah, op. cit., n. 23 above, p. 60.

[87] Ahmed, op. cit., n. 19 above, p. 118. See Maleeha Lodhi and Zahid Hussain, 'General Elections', *Newsline*, October 1990, p. 23.

[88] Shah, op. cit., n. 23 above, p. 60.

[89] Ahmed, op. cit., n. 19 above, p. 118.

[90] Malik, op. cit., n. 6 above, p. 244.

[91] Ahmed, op. cit., n. 19 above, p. 118.

[92] Malik, op. cit., n. 6 above, p. 245.

[93] Ahmed, op. cit., n. 19 above, p. 118.

signalled important changes on the Pakistani political landscape.[94] The provincial assembly elections followed the pattern at the Centre. Besides its overwhelming majority in the Punjab, the IJI formed coalition governments in the NWFP and Baluchistan. In Sind, the PPP obtained only 42 seats, while the MQM won 28 from urban Sind. In other words, the MQM captured almost all the seats in the national and provincial elections of Hyderabad, Sukkur, and Karachi. It was then already enjoying absolute majority in the municipal governments of these cities. The military's handpicked candidate, Jam Sadiq Ali, successfully prevented the formation of a PPP-led provincial government, and an IJI coalition was installed with the support of the MQM and independents.[95] This time, the MQM joined hands with Benazir's and the PPP's opponents.

The Jam Sadiq Government became increasingly dependent on the MQM's backing to counter the PPP. This dependence provided Altaf Hussain the leverage he needed to strengthen the MQM's hold over urban Sind.[96] Ethnic tension increased in Sind as systematic state repression was used by the Jam Sadiq Government to undermine the PPP.[97] Both Jam Sadiq and his successor, Muzaffar Hussain Shah, while heading the IJI–MQM coalition government, gave the MQM a free hand in using violence to contain the PPP. The popular view is that it was done with the consent of the military.[98]

After the death of Jam Sadiq on 4 March 1992, his successor, Syed Muzaffar Hussain Shah, became Chief Minister of Sind. He obtained the cooperation of the MQM and also enjoyed the blessings of the PPP and Jatoi's NPP. It appeared as if Sind was entering a unique phase of cooperation and peace. It was at this stage that Nawaz Sharif wrote a letter to Benazir Bhutto suggesting a dialogue, something that had been long advocated by political circles in the country for the success of a democratic set-up.

[94] Jalal, op. cit., n. 24 above, p. 11.
[95] Kennedy, op. cit., n. 9 above, p. 953.
[96] Ahmed, op. cit., n. 19 above, p. 119.
[97] Ibid., p. 118.
[98] Ibid., pp. 119–20.

However, the effort proved abortive as, a few days later, a new wave of kidnapping hit the headlines in the wake of 'revelations' of armed encounters with the alleged members of Al-Zulfiqar, an organization run by Benazir's brother Murtaza Bhutto. A number of political activists in Sind were reportedly arrested by the provincial government. While the PPP condemned this new wave of repression, the military seemed to be losing patience with the rapid deterioration of law and order. The kidnapping of Mashooq Ali (a close associate of the Aga Khan) in mid-May 1992 brought more pressure for a clean-up operation, and the Army was said to be preparing to launch a large-scale anti-terrorist drive in the troubled southern province of Sind.[99]

By mid-1991, dissent began to surface within the MQM itself. The moderates were antagonized by Hussain's dictatorial leadership, and factions of militants, wanting to extend and expand their influence,[100] desired more space and freedom. The MQM leadership realized that it could never form a government by itself at the national or provincial level, even if it captured all the seats in the assemblies from the areas where the Partition refugees were in a majority. The MQM, therefore, slowly moved towards the national arena and finally changed its name from Muhajir Quami Movement to Muttahida Quami Movement.[101] This decision to join the political mainstream was resented by many party activists, who opposed any move away from regional and ethnic-based mobilization.

By mid-1991, there were violent clashes between MQM loyalists and dissidents in urban Sind. The breaking of ranks within the MQM acquired a new significance.[102] Nawaz Sharif was appointed Prime Minister on an understanding that he would not challenge the military's directions. In return, the military was to outwardly respect civil authority and allow Nawaz the spoils of government. Noticing that the Nawaz-led IJI Government was becoming

[99] Malik, op. cit., n. 6 above, pp. 246–7. See also Derek Brown, 'Pakistani Army to Stamp on Sindh Gangsters', *Guardian*, 20 May 1992.

[100] Ahmed, op. cit., n. 19 above, p. 119.

[101] Mehdi, op. cit., n. 1 above.

[102] Ahmed, op. cit., n. 19 above, p. 119.

increasingly ambitious, the Army Chief of Staff adopted a high public profile and appeared to make a bid for power. There were even apprehensions in IJI circles of a potential military takeover by General Aslam Beg.[103] Beg's retirement in mid-1991 and the appointment of General Asif Nawaz Janjua as Chief of the Army Staff (COAS) was, therefore, welcomed by the IJI, specially as Janjua, as Corps Commander at Karachi, had demonstrated a strong anti-PPP bias.[104] The military was also fearful of the gradual erosion of its authority in Sind in general and in Karachi in particular. Finally, a military operation was launched in Sind.

The crackdown began on 27 May 1992, with mixed reactions from various quarters, though the government and the military chief declared that the operation was directed against gangsters and dacoits and was not an excuse for political reprisals. The MQM was itself taken by surprise, and, in confusion, its MNAs and MPAs (Members of the National Assembly/Provincial Assembly) submitted their resignations and went underground. The operation was widely acclaimed in the Punjab, the seat of military power.[105] Thousands of Hussain's supporters were arrested in conjunction with a propaganda campaign accusing the MQM leadership of criminal and terrorist activities. The army simultaneously assisted a takeover bid by a dissident group led by Afaq Ahmed and Amir Khan. The breakaway group formed a separate party called itself the MQM Haqiqi[106] or the 'Real' MQM. Meanwhile, the military opened a dialogue with the MQM hoping for an agreement on a reconstructed leadership which would exclude Hussain. But their

[103] Ibid., p. 119. See Zahid Hussain, 'Saddam Storm', *Newsline*, February 1991, p. 22.

[104] Ibid., p. 119. Overseeing the exchange of APMSO and PSF (Peoples Student Federation) hostages as Corps Commander, Karachi, Asif Nawaz Janjua told PPP leaders: 'You people are totally immature and therefore incapable of running a government'; Naeem Ahmed Goraya, 'And now, General Janjua', *Newsline*, July 1991, p. 42.

[105] Malik, op. cit., n. 6 above, p. 247.

[106] Ahmed, op. cit., n. 19 above, p. 120. See Zahid Hussain, 'The President vs. the Army', *Newsline*, July 1992, pp. 23–4; and Mohammad Hanif 'MQM: The Hour of Reckoning', *Newsline*, July 1992, pp. 30–2.

Haqiqi protégés failed to acquire a constituency of their own, and no MQM leader could openly oppose Hussain, whose popularity had been reinforced by the military's excesses against party activists. In an attempt to appease the Muhajirs and to obtain their support, the army decided to extend its Operation Blue Fox to rural Sind.

The military operation was started at the behest of the army and presidency and Sharif tried to take credit for sacrificing his coalition interests in order to bring stability and peace in the province. However, corruption, torture and violence remained undiminished in Sind. The editor of a leading magazine wrote: 'Nowhere is the unholy link between crime and politics so marked as in Sind. Political parties in the province have become a heaven for criminals and political power is their shield against the law.'[107] The military's intervention resulted in increasing ethnic unrest and political instability in both urban and rural Sind. The Sind operation also heightened tension in civil-military relations.[108]

The death of General Asif Nawaz Janjua in November 1993 and appointment of General Abdul Waheed Kakar as the new army chief heightened tension between the IJI Government and the military. The new army chief's nomination was vehemently opposed by Nawaz Sharif. Meanwhile, tussles between President Ishaq Khan and Nawaz Sharif also increased on a wide range of issues, such as the controversial Eighth Amendment to the Constitution, and forthcoming presidential elections.

These developments took place at a time when the opposition had closed ranks and launched a movement for Nawaz's resignation and holding of fresh elections. President Ghulam Ishaq decided to seek the opposition's backing for his re-election. Reaching an understanding with the PPP-led opposition, the President dissolved the Nawaz Government on 18 April 1993 on charges of corruption, abuse of power, and attempting to subvert the military's authority.[109]

[107] Malik, op. cit., n. 6 above, p. 247. See also Razia Bhatti, 'Editor's Note', *Newsline*, August 1992, p. 11.

[108] Ahmed, op. cit., n. 19 above, p. 120. See Maleeha Lodhi and Zahid Hussain, 'Power-play in Islamabad', *Newsline*, June 1992, p. 29.

[109] Ibid., p. 121; Zahid Hussain, 'Ishaq Strikes Again', *Newsline*, April 1993, p. 28.

The caretaker government of Prime Minister Balakh Sher Mazari was placed under PPP control and elections announced for July. The IJI Government challenged the dissolution of its government in the Supreme Court. The tussle continued between the President and the Prime Minister and the Nawaz Government, which had been restored by the court, was dismissed once again on 18 July 1993. But this time, the President also had to leave. The agreement was brokered by the Army Chief. A new caretaker government under Prime Minister Moeen Qureshi was established and fresh dates for elections were announced. The elections were held in October 1993.

The October election of 1993 presented a hung Parliament at the Centre. Neither did the PPP nor did the Pakistan Muslim League (PML [N]) and their respective allies win clear majorities.[110] The outcome of elections in Sind was determined by the level and direction of the military's intervention. Although the military did not interfere in the election process in rural Sind, its anti-MQM policies, including restrictions on the party's election activities, prompted threats of boycott by Hussain's group. When Hussain's last-minute effort to negotiate his differences with the Sind military command failed, a boycott call was issued by his party. The MQM boycott helped the PPP and the PML (N) to obtain a number of seats in urban Sind, even though it did not succeed in completely delegitimizing the election process since the voter turnout in Karachi and Hyderabad was reasonable.[111] Threatened with political isolation, the MQM decided to participate in the provincial assembly elections, where the PPP won 56 seats from rural Sind and the MQM obtained 27 from its constituencies. Thus, the MQM emerged as Sind's second-largest party, showing that in urban Sind, it was still a power to reckon with. The MQM supported Benazir Bhutto in her bid for Premiership and she became Prime Minister on 19 October 1993. The MQM also voted for the election of Farooq Leghari, the

[110] Ibid., p. 123. Benazir Bhutto obtained 121 seats to Nawaz Sharif's 72.

[111] Ibid. The turnout in Karachi and Hyderabad was 17 per cent as compared to 27 per cent in rural Sindh.

PPP candidate for the country's presidency. There were reasons for such a position.

Facing the military's hostility and deprived of a chance to influence events at the centre, the MQM decided to regain the political initiative by negotiating a power-sharing arrangement with the PPP in return for its support for the PPP presidential candidate.[112] However, the MQM's rehabilitation continued to depend on the military's approval. During the talks on power-sharing, for example, Sind's newly installed Chief Minister, Abdullah Shah visited Islamabad, where he was presented a military briefing on the Sind situation. The military's decision to withhold its assent for a political role for the Hussain group was, therefore, to determine Benazir Bhutto's policies towards the MQM. This was demonstrated by the PPP's rejection of demands for the withdrawal of charges against the MQM leadership on the grounds that the matter was in the hands of the military and the courts.[113]

The MQM accused the PPP of dithering over fulfilling of its promise, specially in allocation of ministerial portfolios, and pressed continuously for the end of military operations in Karachi.[114] The PPP Government failed to reach a power-sharing agreement with the MQM largely due to the military's insistence on the exclusion of Hussain. As such, once again, there was exacerbation of ethnic tensions in urban Sind.

Indeed, 1994 was one of the darkest years in the history of Pakistan. The single major cause of anxiety was extensive lawlessness in Karachi.[115] In 1994, in the first four months, 31 persons were killed in police custody or in so-called police encounters. Not a single responsible official was taken to task nor any official inquiry made public.[116] According to the Human Rights Commission of

[112] Ibid., pp. 123–4. See Zahid Hussain, 'End of an Era', *Newsline*, November/December 1993, pp. 43–4.

[113] O. Tohid, 'Reluctant Partners', *Newsline*, November/December 1993, p. 61.

[114] Malik, op. cit., n. 6 above, p. 250.

[115] A.B.S. Jafri, *Karachi: A City Refuses to Surrender*, Karachi: Royal Book Company, 1995, p. 409.

[116] Ibid., p. 407.

Pakistan Report, extrajudicial killings, often in the form of staged 'police encounters' in which the police or military shot and killed suspects, many of them unarmed, continued in 1994. Most of these killings occurred in rural Sind, forming part of the army's law and order programme under its clean-up operation which ended on 30 November. On 3 May, the police killed five men in Sukkur. The Sind province investigation determined that the men were rounded up, brought to a police clerk's residence, tied up, and killed with automatic weapons in a well-planned operation. The government denied this allegation. According to government officials and the police, all five were 'dangerous criminals' wanted by law enforcement agencies. Altaf Hussain and some local leaders of the MQM claimed that all five were MQM activists and they were shot and killed in 'cold blood' in the politically motivated operation. The police claimed that there was a serious encounter between the police and these terrorists, but no encounter had actually taken place. The HRCP reported 23 extrajudicial deaths in Sind between January and May. Many were believed to have died as a result of police torture. The Government did not charge or try any law enforcement personnel for these killings. On 29 April 1994, 13 people were killed and 87 injured during police clashes with MQM demonstrators. The Sind Government told the Assembly that 408 persons had been killed in Karachi between November 1993 and mid-December 1994. According to the Edhi Trust, which worked tirelessly to pick up dead bodies from the streets and transport the wounded to hospitals, the number of deaths from January till 31 October was 705, and that 63 members of the law enforcing agencies were killed. One newspaper put the figure at 748 and another at 1,105.[117]

The situation in Karachi took a very violent turn in early December 1994 when the army was withdrawn from the streets of Karachi. Prime Minister Benazir Bhutto interpreted the withdrawal as a sign of return of normalcy in the city after a very long time and hastened to take the credit for it. However, within a few days, hundreds of Karachi's residents died through sniper fire

[117] Ibid., pp. 378–98, 403–9.

following ethnic and sectarian clashes. This turned out to be the worst spell of violence and bloodshed ever witnessed in the city. The PPP regime blamed the Indian intelligence agency Research and Analysis Wing (RAW). The squabbles between the Hussain and Haqiqi factions, combined with Shia–Sunni conflict brought the paramilitary forces back to the city.[118]

There was a little respite for the city during the opening months of 1995. The situation was compounded by the Sunni–Shia conflicts, which gained new momentum, and a fresh wave of sectarian violence saw attacks on mosques and *imambaras*: 25 people were killed by unknown assailants in two incidents on 25 February alone. The next month, the attention of the world was drawn to the city following the killings of two US consular officials in broad daylight on 8 March.[119] In May 1995, the sectarian violence subsided, but ethnic turmoil took a new turn. The security forces confronted MQM supporters. In early June, the situation deteriorated with the explosion of a car bomb outside the provincial assembly building and a military post for the first time. Such a new pattern of violence underlined the inability of the civil and military authorities to curb violence.[120] Rocket launchers were also fired at the Pakistan Television Station and Liaquatabad Police Station. The MQM had the upper hand in what amounted to be an insurgency until the end of June, after which concerted action by security forces, involving extrajudicial means, made inroads into the militant strongholds of Orangi, Korangi, and Gulbahar.

The almost total alienation of the Muhajir population from both the provincial government of Chief Minister Abdullah Shah and the federal authorities was rooted in the excesses of law and order enforcement during the clean-up operation. The PPP leadership in Sind continued to oppose dialogue with the MQM and dubbed it a terrorist organization. Karachi's problems were to be solved through the time-tested law and order machinery and not through political methods.[121]

[118] Malik, op. cit., n. 6 above, p. 250.

[119] Talbot, op. cit., n. 7 above, p. 342.

[120] Malik, op. cit., n. 6 above, p. 251.

[121] Ibid., p. 343.

While the MQM demanded the withdrawal of cases against Altaf Hussain and other underground leaders, the PPP refused to negotiate with the MQM.[122] Following the killing of the American consulate staff, the presidency at Islamabad began to support the idea of a negotiated settlement,[123] and by early July the MQM (A) changed its own hardline attitude. Talks began in the National Assembly building in Islamabad. The change of heart stemmed partly from the growing success of the government's counter-terrorist activities, personally directed by the Interior Minister, Naseerullah Babar. It was also prompted by the way in which the PML (N) and other opposition parties had distanced themselves from the MQM following the launching of its May insurgency. However, little progress could be made, as both sides raised their conflicting 21-point and 18-point charge-sheets.[124] The dialogue did not advance beyond the abortive 10-point agreement of 19 October 1994 between the MQM (A) and the Sind Government.

It was clear by August that although the Government had achieved some success in breaking the networks of MQM (A) militants, the MQM's grassroots public support remained intact.[125] Altaf Hussain, along with his condemnation of Benazir Bhutto, demanded a separate province in urban Sind, and observed: 'They are hunting Muhajirs like birds and animals. They have a license to kill.'[126] Short of criticizing the army, he pursued a dual policy of militant assertion and personal expediency as manifested through nationalist claims for a stable Pakistan. Benazir Bhutto would hit back at the MQM with allegations of daily occurrences of violence in the city. The movement apparently increased pressure for the acceptance of its growing number of demands by the government. Meanwhile, the opposition actively sought support from Altaf Hussain. On 11 June 1995, the PPP Government retaliated by instituting 160 cases of corruption and misconduct (including

[122] Ibid., p. 251.

[123] Talbot, op. cit., n. 7 above, p. 343.

[124] Ibid., p. 344; A. Siddiqui, 'Sparring with the Enemy', *Newsline*, July 1995, pp. 29–30.

[125] Ibid.

[126] Malik, op. cit., n. 6 above, p. 251.

treason) against Nawaz Sharif, and it appeared that all avenues of reconciliation and peaceful negotiation among the various parties in the conflict had been closed.[127] Simultaneously, Benazir refused to initiate talks with Altaf Hussain until his organization laid down its arms, surrendered criminals, and condemned terrorism.[128] Similarly, the opposition continually reiterated its pious sentiments for a dialogue, whereas the religious parties remained totally sidelined or engaged in sectarian rivalries. The PPP and MQM were engaged in an unending power struggle. Karachi's violence thus continued unabated during the second half of 1995—the body count between late August and early November alone stood at 500.

In December 1995, Nasir Hussain, elder brother of Altaf Hussain, was kidnapped and murdered by unknown assailants. Two weeks later, Syed Ahsan Shah, the Sind Chief Minister's brother, was killed in Karachi's Federal B. Area. After the death of these two, a return to relative normalcy began. But this was only for a while. The killings began again. In 1995, more than 1,700 persons, including more than 200 law enforcement personnel, were killed in Karachi.[129] By the end of the year, the Benazir Government was dismissed.

Fresh elections were held in February 1997. The PPP's success was confined to rural Sind and the MQM was the winner in urban Sind. However, the fact is that the PPP won the national and provincial assembly seats in Karachi, Sukkur, Larkana and other towns and cities as well. The PML (N) won seats in Karachi and in some small towns as well as in the rural areas of Sind. The elections in Sind were clearly fought on ethnic lines. The MQM won only the Muhajir-dominated constituencies, and the PPP won the predominantly Sindhi–Baluchi constituencies. However, the PML (N)'s astonishing success mitigated the ethnic polarization in the elections to some extent. Its winning candidates were

[127] Ibid., p. 252.

[128] Ibid., p. 253.

[129] Hosain Yaseer, 'Who Done It?', *Newsline*, November 1995, pp. 46–8.

Sindhi-, and Urdu- or Punjabi-speaking.[130] After the elections, the PML (N) emerged victorious at the centre and Nawaz Sharif became Prime Minister for the second time. The MQM once again became coalition partners in the Sind provincial government. They obtained the release of many of the party's jailed militants, as well as monetary compensation for the families of those killed during the previous regime. But the MQM–Muslim League agreement came to an end soon enough. It was followed by renewed terror on the streets of Karachi and by the government's iron-handed response.[131]

The situation in Karachi seems to have improved somewhat since General Pervez Musharraf came to power in Pakistan on 12 October 1999. Being from Delhi himself, and being an Indian migrant having deep links with Karachi and also being the Commander-in-Chief of the Armed Forces with a firm grip on Pakistan's notorious intelligence agencies, Musharraf has, to some extent, succeeded in controlling and containing violence in Karachi. He has also obtained the support of the most important political force of urban Sind, the MQM. Admittedly, Karachi has suffered a number of terrorist attacks during Musharraf's regime as well, but these are the fallout of 9/11, and have little to do with the dynamics of the ethnic and political complexities of Karachi. Further, sectarian violence since October 1998 has not, as earlier, targeted any particular migrant community of the city or country.[132] It is interesting to note that while the MQM has emerged as the third-largest political party of Pakistan after the PPP and PML and has distinct positions on federation–province relations, feudalism and tribalism, the military's role in politics and on the causes of the marginalization of the masses, it is widely projected by its critics, the Pakistani media and religious and ethnic leaders as a fascist, terrorist, and violent urban group created by the military in Pakistan.

After the meteoric rise of the MQM on Pakistan's political

[130] Ahmed, op. cit., n. 2 above, p. 150.

[131] Akhund, op. cit., n. 31 above, p. 284.

[132] Mehdi, op. cit., n. 1 above.

landscape, many social issues interfacing with the ethnic question have come into sharp focus, and many myths have been woven around and propagated about the MQM and Altaf Hussain's personal life. These tend to muddy the political role of the MQM as well as Hussain. The popular perception of the non-Muhajirs in Pakistan is that the MQM was created, used and punished by the same forces that it was nurtured by—the civil and military establishments since Zia's days—and the MQM enjoyed official patronage of the Zia regime through State-led intelligence agencies. According to Chaudhri Nisar Ali, an IJT minister in the Nawaz cabinet, it was General Aslam Beg and the ISI who brought the MQM to the IJT fold and conspired to destabilize the Benazir Bhutto Government, and that the MQM was used as a pawn. In 1995, a number of Pakistanis believed that Altaf Hussain and his associates in London were being financed and manipulated by the Indian intelligence agencies. On several occasions, it has been portrayed by its numerous opponents as a terrorist organization working for the Indian RAW and the former KGB to destabilize Pakistan.

According to the JI, the MQM is simply a lingual group and nothing else, spreading hatred, whereas the frontier-based Awami National Party (ANP) was viewed as a pro-Kabul and pro-Moscow party with a soft corner for Delhi.[133] The prominent Pakistani religious leader and former chief of the Muttahida Majlis-e-Amal (MMA), Late Shah Ahmed Noorani opposed both the MQM and Sindhi nationalists for 'sabotaging' Islam and Pakistan through language- and tribe- or territory-based schisms. The JI has always regarded the MQM as simply a mischief-mongering *lissani* (lingual, in a derogatory sense) group out to destroy Pakistan.

The MQM's initial emphasis on the issue of Muhajir identity alienated a number of opinion groups in the country which generally referred to it as 'Muhajir chauvinism'. At different times, the demand for separation of urban areas from rural Sind and its designation as Muhajir *subah* would follow the demand for a separate city-state of Karachi or its internationalization as a new

[133] Malik, op. cit., n. 6 above, p. 211.

'Hong Kong'. This did generate speculation and periodic controversies that have disheartened many moderate Urdu-speakers and alienated other communities from MQM-led Muhajir politics.

The MQM has used propaganda techniques such as mass rallies, strikes, posters, graffiti, printed literature, audio and videocassettes to maintain its closed net-work. It fought against the stereotype of Partition refugees as docile and timid, using militancy and violence bordering on fascism to demolish such humiliating caricatures.

In 1994–5, the MQM was perceived to be on the warpath against the authorities and other ethnic plural communities in Karachi. It was blamed for causing daily deaths because of its increased militancy and its discreet attacks on the non-Muhajir communities. The dead bodies sent from Karachi across the country further eroded its image. It is also blamed for pursuing urban guerrilla activities such as car bombs, rocket attacks and even open armed encounters and condemned for initiating a discreet campaign in 'ethnic cleansing' against non-Urdu-speakers, members of law-enforcement agencies and its critics from the media and society at large.

In 1995, the MQM fought street battles with the police and security agencies and it was officially labelled a terrorist organization. Its volatile relations with all other ethnic groups in Sind reflected the absence of a well-considered strategy and an unrealistic dependence on emotional appeal and street violence. By denigrating Sindhis, Punjabis, Baluchis and Pushtoons, the MQM entered into a perennial state of war with the parallel ethnic communities, and, according to many observers, Karachi became Pakistan's Beirut largely due to the criminalization of ethnic dissent attributed to Altaf Hussain.[134] It was alleged that the MQM hit-men selected civilian and paramilitary targets in Karachi and used rockets, car bombs and machine guns to kill the maximum number of persons,[135] and that its armed bands engaged in sniping, looting and kidnapping in Hyderabad in October 1998.

[134] Ibid., p. 205–46.

[135] Ibid., p. 116, Ch. 10, fn. 7.

It is also alleged that the press was blackmailed by strong-arm tactics adopted by the MQM, including reprimands, kidnapping, and terrorist acts performed by well-organized groups of armed men. The MQM is said to have intimidated dissidents and independent journalists including correspondents and editors of the daily *Dawn*, *Jang*, *Herald* and *Newsline*, the BBC's correspondent in Karachi. The MQM's problems with Salah-ud-din, the pro-JI editor of the weekly *Takbeer* during 1991 also merit special mention.

Nevertheless, Hussain remains the undisputed leader of the organization and maintains contacts with various forces in the country. For a long time, Hussain has remained the focal point through a combination of charisma, propaganda machinations and the highly disciplined structure of the movement. Muhajirs consider Altaf Hussain as a 'Messiah' for the removal of their grievencies. He is the undisputed leader of the community and his powerful position in urban Sind politics was duly recognized by the Prime Ministers, Chief Ministers and bureaucrats during 1988–98, in particular. The MQM is a strong coalition partner in General Pervez Musharraf's government. By raising slogans against feudalism and *sardari* system in Pakistan, calling for just sharing of power and resources among provinces and liberating 98 per cent of the people of Pakistan from poverty and depriviation, Altaf Hussain has clearly emerged as a leader of the downtrodden.

The MQM leadership denies the charges levelled against it. It condemns the so-called religious leaders and ethnic groups for their campaign to tarnish the image of a modern, populist and progressive party. It claims that it is struggling to bring about the empowerment of the downtrodden people in a country dominated by the Generals, bureaucrats, feudals and tribals.

Whether one is closer to the viewpoint of the advocates or to the critics of the MQM, one has to acknowledge that the party has given a new voice, a strong leadership, and a new direction to the faceless, voiceless, docile and vulnerable Partition refugees.

Conclusion

This study covering different aspects of forced migration due to the Partition of India in August 1947 and after has tried to highlight the circumstances under which the Indian Muslims moved with their family members and friends and settled down in different parts of Pakistan. It was a human issue posing a great challenge to the country during its early years.

The newly-created country was in chaos, its treasury was empty, it did not have organized civilian structures and there was violence, uncertainty and gloom, but Pakistan, under the leadership of Governor-General Mohammed Ali Jinnah and Prime Minister Liaquat Ali Khan geared up the administrative machinery of the emergent state to deal with the challenges. The State responded positively to the problems of managing the waves of incoming refugees.

The main problem was to create space for these people and to secure an early and orderly evacuation and settlement of the refugees as soon as possible as the greatest migration in history was under way. Pakistan welcomed the new arrivals and dealt with them systematically. Issues relating to refugee management, rehabilitation, resettlement, distribution of evacuee property and grant of citizenship were gradually dealt with and the issue of reintegration of the refugees with society and their involvement in the political and electoral networks and systems addressed.

The refugees were gradually integrated within the new State. With their involvement in the movement for Pakistan and proximity to the leaders of the movement, their mobility and ethnic cohesion, high percentage of literacy and a strong survival instinct, the Partition refugees emerged as ruling partners of Pakistan. This was strengthened by the designation of their language, Urdu, as the national language. They were thus empowered. They played an important role in political and economic development programmes and joined the bureaucracy, judiciary, the Armed Forces, business ventures and the emerging civil society. During the first decade of Pakistan (1947–57), Karachi remained the centre of political and economic activity. During this decade, the refugees got settled and began normal life in an environment which was not hostile.

But the Muhajir culture, in most of its important manifestations, was different from the indigenous political culture. It is true that the Partition refugees who came from Indian Punjab or the state of Jammu and Kashmir assimilated with ease in Pakistani Punjab. They spoke the same language (Punjabi) and cherished the Punjabi culture and way of life. But the refugees who came from UP, CP, Bihar, West Bengal, Bombay, and Gujarat and settled down in urban Sind were different from the local Sindhis. These two were products of two very different political cultures. A clash between them was virtually inevitable, and cracks began to appear soon. The newcomers to the city of Karachi were infatuated with their leaders and did not welcome the military regime of Ayub Khan. A tussle for power surfaced soon after and fierce competition began between the locals and non-locals. This period also saw the first glimmerings of disquiet of the Partition refugees. Ayub adopted very dubious policies against the Urdu-speaking refugees settled in Sind. Their power and influence were systematically curtailed, Karachi being the worst affected. He shifted the capital from Karachi to Islamabad and encouraged Punjabis and Pathans to start businesses.

During his reign, green revolution technologies were introduced in the agriculture sector resulting in a mass exodus of peasants and small landowners, mostly from Punjab. They moved to Karachi and employment opportunities for the refugees gradually shrank. Ayub also dismissed prominent Partition refugees from important positions in the bureaucracy, replacing them with locals. The Muhajirs were adversely affected by the military takeover, which had launched a policy of discrimination.

The government of General Yahya Khan followed the same pattern and adopted certain inimical policies which created more disparities and tussles between locals and refugees in Sind, curtailing employment opportunities, prompting discontent and causing alienation. It was a period of great stress for the Partition refugees. They were dismayed and disturbed and were disliked by the military dictators.

After the dismemberment of Pakistan in 1971, clashes and conflicts between the Partition refugees and the local wielders of power became inevitable. Every nationality and community started clamouring for its rights. The country was passing through another difficult period of domestic turmoil, and the question of national identity remained unresolved in the post-1971 era. In fact, the issue as to whether Pakistanis should consider themselves as Pakistanis first and Sindhis, Baluchis, Punjabis or Pathans afterwards still remains a contentious issue.

In Sind, in particular, Sindhi nationalism became very assertive during the Premiership of Zulfiqar Ali Bhutto. Initially, the Sindhis had very warmly welcomed the Partition refugees hoping for peaceful coexistence with them and in sharing the citizenship of a newly Independent State. When those Partition refugees became empowered and got higher ranks in the civil bureaucracy, the Sindhi elite felt hindrances in career advancement, employment and other economic opportunities. The Sindhi alienation and deprivation clearly got aggravated when the local Sindhis were almost purged from Karachi. They were hardly in the corridors of power any more. It naturally gave rise to clashes between the Sindhis and Partition refugees. The Sindhis had reached the conclusion that Pakistan's Urdu-speaking elite wouldn't allow them to participate in the state machinery, in prosperity and in the decision-making processes. The Sindhis in the 1970s perceived Urdu as a major cultural threat to Sindhi ethnic identity.

These developments led to ethnic tension and the Sindhis demanded more autonomy. When Bhutto came to power, hope was aroused for a better future among the Sindhis who began to feel for the first time that they were participating in the political processes of the country. Under Bhutto's regime, the Sindhis occupied some jobs in the nationalized sector, but the introduction of a quota system and promotion of Sindhi language in Karachi caused a feeling of marginalization among the Partition refugees. They felt isolated and left out.

During the Zia era, the Muhajirs were exploited badly by the government and intelligence agencies, including the ISI. The Zia regime adopted almost deliberate pro-Muhajir and anti-Sindhi policies, promoted the depoliticization of the masses, and divided the province into *biradaris*, sects, and ethnic and linguistic groups.

In certain respects, migration had not affected Punjab as critically as Sind. Most of the Muslim Punjabis settled down in Pakistani Punjab. They shared the same culture, language and history and adjusted themselves easily. But in Sind, the situation was different. The Urdu-speaking people felt superior, thought that they belonged to the elite class and deserved special rights and privileges. Contrarily, the State systematically disempowered them.

By the 1980s, ethnic tension was at a peak in Sind. Demographic changes were taking place in urban Sind. There were conflicts between the Punjabis, Afghan refugees, Biharis, and local Sindhis. The emergence of a powerful Sindhi nationalist movement caused the revitalization of Muhajir ethnic mobilization. Competition over jobs and domination of squatter settlements, along with easy access to sophisticated arms—a fallout of the Afghan war—pervaded the culture of terrorism from Karachi to the Khyber.

By the mid-1980s, violent clashes began between the Muhajirs and Pathans in urban Sind. A new generation of Sindhi and Muhajir leadership not averse to militancy and ethnic contentions became increasingly powerful in the absence of political platforms. It was under these circumstances that the MQM emerged on Pakistan's political landscape to fight for the rights of different generations of Partition refugees. The creation of the MQM was a new factor in Pakistani politics, dominated as it was by feudal and tribal overlords and by the civil and military bureaucracy. The political scene witnessed the arrival of leaders belonging to the middle class.

Under Altaf Hussain's leadership, the MQM impacted decisively on the politics of Pakistan. It put forward a claim for the migrants to be designated as a fifth nationality. Despite their privileged position, since Partition, the Urdu-speaking people had not claimed to be a separate nationality from 1947 to 1984. However, their leaders frequently complained that every government which came to power after Liaquat Ali Khan adopted discriminatory policies against the Muhajirs. They had no identity, position, or job protection. The local citizens presented themselves as Pathans, Punjabis, Sindhis, or Baluchis, but there was no tag for the 'original' Pakistanis.

Hussain explained that Pakistan had been created from the blood of Muhajirs, that the Pakistan movement had been led and sustained by the Muslim-minority areas of undivided India, and that the Muhajirs had a higher stake in Pakistan. However, despite their historical role in the creation of Pakistan, powerful ethnic and regional groups in the corridors of power in Islamabad and Sind resisted the grant of equal status to the Muhajirs. He also asserted in 1984 that the urban centres in Sind were under MQM control, adding that the Muhajirs were a distinct nationality.

The MQM, led by leaders of modest backgrounds, impacted decisively on the politics of Pakistan. Throughout the political merry-go-round characteristic of the Benazir and Nawaz Sharif era, the MQM had aligned with both, but the miseries of the Muhajirs multiplied with every successive government, even though it participated in the 1988, 1990, 1993, 1997 and 2002 elections and emerged as the third most-powerful party in the country and always won a sizeable number of seats in both the Sind Assembly and the Pakistan National Assembly, reaffirming its massive following among Urdu-speakers. The State and its coercive organs were not very kind to the MQM, as the party was raising too many issues and threatening the vital interests of the power elite of the country.

The MQM was subjected to harassment and physical torture. According to it, 15,000 MQM activists and supporters were killed and many were sent to unknown places, while approximately 2,000 Muhajirs, including prominent members of provincial and national assemblies were imprisoned in the 1990s. Apart from that, the Rangers, police, frontier constabulary and 3,000 plainclothes intelligence men were reportedly deputed to suppress the Muhajirs. The elected governments always exploited and betrayed them for their own advantages and treated them as aliens and the MQM often failed to achieve as much as it hoped to gain by joining the government. Urban Sind became a sort of battlefield, where violent clashes took place between Partition refugees and the police, Rangers, political parties, and rival ethnic groups.

The government and its organs and a number of leading newspapers, on the other hand, condemned the MQM for indulging in terrorist activities, including car bombings, rocket attacks and open armed encounters. It was also blamed for undertaking a discreet ethnic cleansing campaign against non-Urdu-speakers, members of law enforcement agencies and its critics in the media and elsewhere. These circumstances fuelled ethnicity in Sind. Ethnic politics certainly took a bad turn during the 1980s and 1990s, with a new generation of ethnic groups assuming militancy in both rural and urban Sind. In 1995, more than 1,700 people, including 200 law enforcement personnel, were killed in the deadly streets of Karachi. The MQM disclaimed any role in such activities and successfully emerged as the sole and authentic representative of the Muhajir community. When criticized for championing the cause of the Muhajirs only, and realizing that the MQM could never form a government by itself at national or provincial level, even if it captured all the seats in the assemblies from the areas where the Partition refugees were in majority, the MQM slowly moved into the wider national arena and finally changed its name from Muhajir Quami Movement to Muttahida Quami Movement (United National Movement). The MQM leaders insisted on a broader definition of Muhajirs, including not only the Urdu-speaking people who migrated from India and their progeny, but also the Punjabis and others who migrated from India and settled down in different areas of Pakistan. It also projected itself as an advocate for the rights of the downtrodden Punjabis, Sindhis, Baluchis, Pathans, Seraikis, Indian migrants and others, for the autonomy of all the four provinces of Pakistan (Sind, Baluchistan, NWFP, and Punjab) and for the Northern Areas, and for abolishing feudalism and tribalism.

Slowly but surely, Hussain and the MQM are now becoming the focal point of all the adversaries of the Punjabi-dominated ruling clique (comprising the Baluchis, Pathans, Sindhis, Seraikis and people of the Northern Areas). Hussain now operates from London, and is reportedly gaining footholds in rural Sind, southern Punjab and Baluchistan, in particular.

Certain questions openly making the rounds in concerned circles of contemporary Pakistan are: What does the future hold for the Partition refugees in Pakistan? Would the Partition refugees become isolationist and campaign for a confederal scheme of things, or even for separation from the rest of Pakistan, or would the refugees strive to grow as part of an all-Pakistan-based nationalist and populist political movement for the rights of all the people of Pakistan, or can the Partition refugees play the role of catalyst in the movement against feudalism, tribalism, militarism and political violence, championing the cause of the common people of the entire country?

It is not easy to answer these questions. Pakistan and the Partition refugees go together. If the principles of power-sharing and resource-sharing are not respected in Pakistan, and if the Partition refugees are further marginalized, then Pakistan would be damaged. Again, if the Partition refugees take another route, do not join the national struggle for the rights of all and take unilateral steps at the cost of Pakistan, then they would critically harm the Partition refugees as well.

The MQM represents an urban, well-educated middle class. There is a good chance that it may become the moving force for forcing Pakistan away from its feudal–tribal order to a more democratic and pluralist society. It may play the role of a catalyst, but then it has to resolve the ethnic discontent through social and economic give and take and build bridges and not walls. The MQM has to emerge as an integrationist party and not a party bulldozing other ethnic elements. It has to carry the diverse ethnic groups with it, and, finally and very importantly, succeed in gaining the trust of all ethnic communities and promoting a democratic political order. In recent times, the MQM has gained a political space in rural Sind, Baluchistan, Punjab as well as the NWFP. It is now campaigning against feudalism and *sardari* system and exposing the feudal hold of the PPP and Muslim League—the two mainstream political parties of Pakistan. Furthermore, the MQM is vigorously campaigning against violence on women and has actively helped and assisted the earthquake victims in the Punjab and Azad Kashmir. It is also opposed to the exploitation of the masses in the name of religion by religious parties. These initiative have considerable appeal and the MQM is now being regarded as a party willing to serve the downtrodden. The party is clearly projecting itself as a party not only of the Muhajirs but one which would also like to serve the Pathans, the Sindhis, the Baluchis, the Punjabis, and the Kashmiris. The party may have a remarkable future ahead if it succeeds in convincing the Pakistan masses that it is not a party for Muhajirs only. However it still has a long way to go.

Abbreviations

APMSO: All Pakistan Muhajir Student Organization, established on 11 June 1978 in reaction to the unilateral policies of the Islami Jamiat-i-Tulaba (IJT).

HRCP: Human Rights Commission of Pakistan.

INA: Indian National Army.

ISI: Inter-Services Intelligence (of Pakistan).

IJI: Islami Jamhouri Ittehad. Islamic Democracy Alliance, a coalition of nine right wing pro-Islamic and anti-PPP parties led by Nawaz Sharif, formed in 1988 under the guidance of the military's intelligence (ISI).

IJT: Islami Jamiat-i-Tulaba. An Islamic student organization, the student wing of the Jamaat-i-Islami, having a hold on campuses in the late 1980s.

JI: Jamaat-i-Islami. Pakistan's most active Islamic political party.

JSM: Jiye Sindh Movement or Sindh National Front (SNF): a political movement run by G.M. Syed, the veteran Sindhi politician.

MEO: Military Evacuation Organisation.

MMA: Muttahida Majlis-e-Amal (a religious–political party).

MQM (A): MQM Altaf group.

MQM Haqiqi: Real MQM, a rebel group of the MQM.

MRD: Movement for the Restoration of Democracy, a broad-based party coalition dominated by the PPP, set up in February 1981 under the leadership of Nusrat Bhutto (Bhutto's wife) to demand the end of martial law and the holding of elections under the terms of the 1973 Constitution.

NPP: National People's Party, a political organization formed by Ghulam Mustafa Jatoi, one of the biggest *wadera* (landlords) of Sind and co-founder of the Pakistan Peoples Party.

PML (N): Pakistan Muslim League (Nawaz Sharif group).

PPI: Punjabi-Pushtoon Ittehad. Punjabi and Pathan Alliance, a political party formed in 1987 by Punjabi leader Ghulam Sarwar Awan.

RSS: Rashtriya Swayamsevak Sangh, a Hindu fundamentalist or cultural group.

SNA: Sindh National Alliance, established in 1988 by G.M. Syed, the veteran Sindhi politician, an organization which brought together various ideological groups.

ASSP: Anjuman-i-Sipah-e-Sahaba Party, a Sunni terrorist organization financed by Saudi Arabia and the US.

AZ: Al-Zulfiqar, a political organization run by Benazir's brother Murtaza Bhutto.

Glossary

90 (Nine Zero): political secretariat.

Akali Dal: the Sikh organization.

Akalis: Sikh followers of the Akali Dal.

atta: coarse flour of wheat.

Azizabad: a middle-class area of Karachi Central where '90' is situated.

Bara Market: Pushtoon smugglers' market.

biradari: brotherhood, family, or household.

chapatti: a flat unleavened bread.

charpoy: a light bedstead.

dal: pulses.

Deobandis and Barelvis: different sects of Sunni Muslims, i.e.'those from, or affiliated to Deoband' (a town in India's UP, where a leading seminary is located) and 'those affiliated to Bareilly' (a city in India's UP, where another leading seminary is located).

dhoti: a piece of clothing worn wrapped around the waist and covering the legs, fastened behind after passing between the legs.

Edhi Trust: The Edhi welfare foundation is run by Abdul Sattar Edhi, known as the 'Angle of Mercy'. It helps the needy, poor, hungry, homeless, sick, mentally retarded and down trodden people of Pakistan.

Abdul Sattar Edhi Trust was founded in 1953, and later in 1978 became the Edhi Foundation. The foundation provides a variety of services to ordinary people who may not get help elsewhere through its 250 centres spread across the country.

Federal B. Area: a middle-class area of Karachi Central.

imambara: mosque of Shia Muslims, the place to which the *taziya* and standard *alam* are conveyed and kept in the month of Moharram.

kirpan: a long knife, or sword generally kept by Sikhs for self-defence.

Muhajir: refugee.

Muhajireen or Partition refugees: Muhajir is the term which was used by the Muslims of Bihar, UP, CP, Delhi and Bengal who migrated to newly created Pakistan from northern India and settled in Karachi, Hyderabad and interior Sind. The Muhajir community comprises Gujaratis, Hyderabadis, Madrasis, Khojas, Ghanchees, Kutchis, Memons, Urdu-speaking Bengalis, Biharis and descendants of migrants from UP and Delhi.

Mukti Bahini: Bengali freedom fighters group (a guerrilla organization).

panahguzeen: refugees; asylum seekers.

Partition refugees: mainly Urdu-speaking people of undivided India who migrated to Pakistan during Partition.

razai: a quilt stuffed with cotton; a very light handmade blanket.

sari: a common garment of women of Indian subcontinent which is a long piece of cloth wrapped around the lower body and draped around the torso, worn with a blouse.

sarkanda huts: huts made of elephant grass.

shahidi jathas: suicide squads of Sikh bands armed with firearms, swords, daggers, etc.

Sohrab Goth: semi-independent settlement of Pushtoon and Afghan population, a den of the drug mafia outside the city of Karachi.

subah: province.

Bibliography

PRIMARY SOURCES

Afzal, Rafi Quem, *Speeches and Statements of Quaid-i-Azam Mohammad Ali Jinnah: 1911–34, 1947–48*, Lahore: Research Society of Pakistan, 1966.

Bhutto, Zulfiqar Ali, *Speeches and Statements*, Lahore: Classic Publishers.

Government of Pakistan, *Chronology of Pakistan June 1947–June 1953*, Karachi: Kamal Publications.

———, *Treaty Series 1947*, Karachi: Government of Pakistan, 1955.

———, *Treaty Series 1948*, Karachi: Government of Pakistan, 1955.

———, *Treaty Series: Treaties and International Agreement Entered in to by the Government of Pakistan*, Karachi: Government of Pakistan, 1955.

———, *The First Five-Year Plan, 1955–60*, Karachi: Government of Pakistan, 1956.

———, *Ten Years of Pakistan: 1947–1957*, Karachi: Government of Pakistan, 1957.

———, *Struggle for Independence: 1857–1947*, Karachi: Government of Pakistan, 1958.

———, *Joint Communiqués: 14 August 1947–December 1957*, Islamabad: Government of Pakistan, 1977.

House of Representatives Committee of Foreign Affairs, USA, *Report of the Special Mission to the Middle East, South and Southeast Asia and the Western Pacific*, Washington, D.C.: House of Representatives Committee, 1956.

Khan, Ayub, *Speeches and Statements*, Karachi: Government of Pakistan, vols. 1–9.

Rafique, M., *Speeches and Statements of Quaid-e-Millat Liaquat Ali Khan (1941–51)*, Lahore: Research Society of Pakistan, 1967.

Siddiqui, Mohammad, *Speeches of Quaid-i-Azam Mohammad Ali Jinnah*, Karachi: Quaid-i-Azam Academy, 1973.

Umar, Mohammad, *Rare Speeches of Quaid-e-Azam Mohammad Ali Jinnah, 1910–1918*, Karachi: Sukkur Publishers, Al-Mahfooz Research Academy, 1973.

SECONDARY SOURCES

Books

Aaiwan, K.H., *Elections in Pakistan*, Karachi: Mehran Press, 1991.

Abdullah, Ahmed, *The Historical Background of Pakistan and its People*, Karachi: Tanzeem Publishers, 1973.

Afzal, M. Rafique, *Political Parties in Pakistan: 1947–1958*, Islamabad: National Institute of Historical and Cultural Research, 1976–86.

———, *Political Parties in Pakistan: 1958–1969*, Islamabad: National Institute of Historical and Cultural Research, 1987.

———, *Political Parties in Pakistan: 1969–1971*, Islamabad: National Institute of Historical and Cultural Research, 1998.

Ahmad, Mujeeb, *Jamiyyat Ulama-i-Pakistan: 1948–1979*, Islamabad: National Institute of Historical and Cultural Research, 1993.

Ahmed, Feroz, *Ethnicity and Politics in Pakistan*, Karachi: Oxford University Press, 1998.

Ahmed, Ishtiaq, *State, Nation and Ethnicity in Contemporary South Asia*, London, New York: Cassell, 1996.

Ahmed, Munir, *MQM*, Lahore: Gora Publishers, 1995.

———, *Altaf Hussain*, Lahore: Gora Publishers, 1996.

Akhund, Iqbal, *Trial and Error: The Advent and Eclipse of Benazir Bhutto*, Karachi: Oxford University Press, 2000.

Ali, Chaudhri Mohammad, *The Emergence of Pakistan*, Lahore: Research Society of Pakistan, University of Punjab, 1973.

Ali, K., *A New History of Indo-Pak since 1526*, Dacca: Ali Publications, 1970.

Ali, Mohammad, *Some Economic Problems*, Karachi: University of Karachi, 1954.

———, *Quaid-e-Azam and Muslim Economic Resurgence*, Lahore: Amir Publications, 1977.

Ali, Rahmat Choudhary, *The Fatherland of the Pak Nation*, Lahore: Book Traders, 1946.

Amin, Tahir, *Ethno-National Movement of Pakistan*, Islamabad: Institute of Policy Studies, 1989.

Athar, Khalid, *Safar-i-Zindagi: MQM ki Kahani, Altaf Hussain ki Zabani* (The Story of the MQM, Narrated by Altaf Hussain), Lahore: Jang Publishers, 1998.

Azam, Ikram, *Pakistan's Security and National Integration: A Study in Opinion and Point of View*, Rawalpindi: London Books, 1974.

Aziz, K.K., *Britain and Muslim India*, London: Heinemann, 1963.

———, *Party Politics in Pakistan: 1947–1958*, Islamabad: National Commission of Historical and Cultural Research, 1976.

Aziz, Qutubuddin, *Exciting Stories to Remember: 1948–1994*, Karachi: Islamic Media, 1995.

Bahadur, Kalim, *The Jama'at-i-Islami of Pakistan: Political Thought and Political Action*, Lahore: Progressive Books, 1978.

Burki, Shahid Javed, 'The Roots of Diversity' in *Pakistan: Fifty Years of Nationhood*, ed. Javed Shahid Burki, Lahore: Vanguard Books, 1999.

———, *Pakistan: Fifty Years of Nationhood*, Lahore: Vanguard Books, 1999.

Choudhary, G.W., *Pakistan's Relations with India 1947–66*, London: Pall Mall Press, 1968.

Collins, Larry and Dominique Lapierre, *Freedom at Midnight*, New Delhi: Vikas Publishing, 1976.

Grover, Verinder and Ranjana Arora, *Pakistan: 50 Years of Independence; Towards Independence; the Pre-1944 Period*, New Delhi: Deep and Deep, 1997.

———, *Political System in Pakistan*, vol. 2: *Constitutional Development in Pakistan*, New Delhi: Deep and Deep, 1995.

———, *Political System of Pakistan: Political Parties, Election and Regionalism*, New Delhi: Deep and Deep, 1995.

Dasgupta, Jyoti Bhusan, *Indo-Pakistan Relations 1947–1955*, Amsterdam: Djam Batan, 1958.

Haider, Syed Karim, *Pakistan's General Elections 1991*, Lahore: Pakistan Study Centre, University of Punjab, 1999.

Hodson, H.V., *The Great Divide: Britain–India–Pakistan*, Karachi: Oxford University Press, 1969.

Hussain, Arif, *Pakistan, its Ideology and Foreign Policy*, London: Frank Cass, 1966.

Hussain, Mushahid, *Pakistan's Politics: The Zia Years*, Lahore: Progressive Publishers, 1990.

Hussain, Zahid, *Rationale of Partition*, Karachi: Royal Book Company, 1990.

Jafri, A.B.S., *Behind the Killing Fields of Karachi: A City Refuses to Surrender*, Karachi: Royal Book Company, 1996.

Jalal, Ayesha, *Democracy and Authoritarianism in South Asia: A Comparative and Historical Perspective*, Lahore: Sang-e-Meel Publications, 1995.

Jehan, Rounaq, *Pakistan: Failure in National Integration*, New York, London: Columbia University Press, 1972.

Keesing's Research Report, *Pakistan from 1947 to the Creation of Bangladesh*, New York: Charles Scribner's Sons, 1971.

Kennedy, Charles H., *Pakistan 1992*, Boulder, CO; San Francisco; Oxford: Westview Press; Lahore, Karachi, Islamabad: Pakistan Book Corporation, 1993.

Kennedy, Charles H. and Rasul Bakhsh Rais, *Pakistan 1995–96*, Karachi, Lahore, Islamabad: Vanguards Books, 1995.

Kennedy, Charles H., Kathleen McNeil, Carl Ernst and David Gilmartin, eds., *Pakistan at the Millennium*, Karachi: Oxford University Press, 2003.

Khaliquzzaman, Choudhry, *Pathway to Pakistan*, Lahore: Longmans Green, 1961.

Khan, Mazhar Ali, *Pakistan: The First Twelve Years*, Karachi: Oxford University Press, 1996.

Khan, Mohammad Raza, *What Price Freedom*, Karachi: Kutub Printers, 1977.

Khan, Saleem Ullah, *The Journey to Pakistan: A Documentation of Refugees of 1947*, Islamabad: Natural Documentation Center, 1993.

Khan, Wali, *Facts are Facts: The Untold Story of India's Partition*, Lahore: Vikas Publishing, 1987.

Mahmood, Safdar, *Pakistan: Political Roots and Development*, Lahore: Vanguard Books, 1990.

Malik, Iftikhar H., *State and Civil Society in Pakistan Politics of Authority, Ideology and Ethnicity*, London, New York: Oxford University Press, 1997.

Manzar, Shehzad, *Sindh Kay Nasli Masaeel* (Racial Problems of Sind), Lahore: Fiction House, 1994.

Mirza, Mahmood, *Aaj ka Sindh* (Today's Sind), Lahore: Progressive Publishers, 1986.

Papanek, Gustav F., *Pakistan's Development, Social Goals and Private Incentives*, Cambridge: Harvard University Press, 1967.

Pirzada, Sayyid A.S., *The Politics of the Jamiat Ulema-i-Islam Pakistan: 1971–77*, Karachi: Oxford University Press, 2000.

Qadri, Hafiz Osama, *Jabar, Tashadud aur Sazish* (Violence and Conspiracy), Karachi: Pak Academy, 1998.

———, *Pakistan: Sazish Aur Siyasat* (Pakistan: Conspiracy and Politics), Karachi: Pak Academy, 1999.

Qureshi, Ishtiaq Hussain, *The Struggle for Pakistan*, Karachi: Bureau of Composition, Compilation and Translation, University of Karachi, 1965.

Rahman, Khalid, Muhibul Haq Sahibzada and Mushfiq Ahmed, eds., *Jama'at-e-Islami and National and International Politics*, Islamabad: Book Traders, 1999.

Renwick, Alan and Ian Swinburn, *Basic Political Concepts*, London: Hutchinson, 1980.

Rizvi, Hasan Askari, *Internal Strife and External Intervention*, Lahore: Progressive Publishers, 1981.

———, *The Military 1947–86 and Politics in Pakistan*, Lahore: Progressive Publishers, 1974, 1976, 1986.

Sagah, Tariq Ismail, *Election 90*, Lahore: Maqbool Academy, 1990.

Salamat, Zarina, *Pakistan 1947–1958: An Historical Review*, Islamabad: National Institute of Historical and Cultural Research, 1992.

Saleem, Ahmed, *Muhajir Quami Movement: Tashkeel aur Jaddojahad* (Refugee National Movement: Formation and Endeavours), Lahore: Sarang Publications, 1996.

———, *Solagta Howa Sindh* (Smouldering Sind), Lahore: Jang Publishers, 1990.

Sayeed, Kahlid B., *The Political System of Pakistan*, Lahore, Karachi, Dacca: Oxford University Press, 1967.

Seervai, H.M., *Partition of India: Legend and Reality*, Bombay: Emmenem Publications, 1989.

Shah, Mehtab Ali, *The Foreign Policy of Pakistan: Ethnic Impacts and Diplomacy: 1971–1994*, London, New York: I.B. Tauris, 1997.

Sherwani, Latif Ahmed, *The Partition of India, and Mountbatten*, Karachi: Council for Pakistan Studies, 1986.

Siddiqui, Abdur-Rehman, *Muhajir-Pachas Sala Safar ki Dastan* (Muhajirs: The Story of Fifty Year's Journey), Lahore: Azad Enterprises, 1998.

Singh, Patwant, *The Struggle for Power in Asia*, London: Hutchinson, 1971.

Sohail, Massarrat, *Partition and Anglo-Pakistan Relations: 1947–51*, Lahore, Karachi, Islamabad: Vanguard Books, 1991.

Suleri, Z.A., *Pakistan: Lost Years*, Lahore: Progressive Publishers, 1967.

Talbot, Ian, *Freedom's Cry: The Popular Dimension in the Pakistan Movement and Partition Experience in North-West India*, Karachi: Oxford University Press, 1996.

———, *Pakistan: A Modern History*, Lahore, Karachi, Islamabad: Vanguard Books, 1999.

Vorys, Karl von, *Political Development in Pakistan*, London, Princeton: Oxford University Press, 1965.

Waseem, Mohammad, *Politics and the State in Pakistan*, Lahore: Progressive Publishers, 1989.

———, *The 1993 Elections in Pakistan*, Lahore, Karachi, Islamabad: Vanguard Books, 1994.

Zaidi, Akbar, 'Sindhi vs Mohajir: Contradictions, Conflicts, and Compromises', in *Regional Imbalances and the National Question in Pakistan*, ed. Akbar Zaidi, Lahore: Vanguard Books, 1992.

———, ed., *Regional Imbalances and the National Question in Pakistan*, Lahore, Karachi, Islamabad, Peshawar: Vanguard Books. 1992.

Zia, Shakeel Ahmed, *Sindh ka Muqaddama* (Sind's Lawsuit), Karachi: Muhajir Academy, 1986.

Ziring, Lawerence, *The Ayub Khan Era: Politics in Pakistan, 1958–1969*, New York: Syracuse University Press, 1971.

ARTICLES IN JOURNALS

Ahmad, Mushtaq, 'Pakistan's Economic Relations with the United States', *Pakistan Horizon* (Karachi), vol. IV, no. 1, 1951, pp. 51–8.

———, 'Pakistan and the United Nations', *Pakistan Horizon*, vol. IV, no. 3, 1951, pp. 130–51.

Baqai, I. H., 'Relations between Afghanistan and Pakistan', *Pakistan Horizon*, vol. 1, no. 3, 1948, pp. 206–21.

Begum, Sultana Naema, 'Indo-Pakistan Trade', *Pakistan Horizon*, vol. III, no. 3, 1950, pp. 165–79.

Binder, Leonard, 'The New Constitution of Pakistan and the Treaty-Making Powers', *Pakistan Horizon*, vol. VIII, no. 2, 1955, pp. 351–61.

Birdwood, Lord, 'Pakistan in Global Strategy', *Pakistan Horizon*, vol. VIII, no. 2, 1955, pp. 348–50.

Borton, William, 'Pakistan's Claim to Kashmir', *Foreign Affairs*, vol. 28, no. 3, 1950, pp. 299–308.

Chaudhri, Mohammad Ahsan, 'Pakistan, India and the United States', *Pakistan Horizon*, vol. VI, no. 4, 1953, pp. 171–9.

———'The Relations of Pakistan with Afghanistan', *Pakistan Horizon*, vol. VII, no. 4, 1955, pp. 494–504.

———'Pakistan and the United States', *Pakistan Horizon*, vol. IX, no. 4, 1956, pp. 196–206.

———, 'Evacuee Property in India and Pakistan', *Pakistan Horizon*, vol. X, no. 2, 1957, pp. 96–109.

———, 'Pakistan and the Muslim World', *Pakistan Horizon*, vol. X, no. 3, 1957, pp. 156–66.

Feldman, Herbert, 'Pakistan's Relations with United Kingdom', *Pakistan Horizon*, vol. VIII, no. 3, 1955, pp. 419–28.

Godery, W., 'Anglo-Pakistan Trade', *Pakistan Horizon*, vol. II, no. 4, 1949, pp. 188–98.

Group Study, 'The Fundamentals of Pakistan's Foreign Policy', *Pakistan Horizon*, vol. IX, no. 1, 1956, pp. 37–50.

Hassan, K. Sarwar, 'The Foreign Policy of Mr Liaquat Ali Khan', *Pakistan Horizon*, vol. IV, no. 4, 1951, pp. 181–99.

———, 'Cambell-Johnson's Mission with Mountbatten, *Pakistan Horizon*, vol. V, no. 2, 1952, pp. 96–109.

Jafri, N.R., 'Pakistan's Trade with India', *Pakistan Horizon*, vol. V, no. 2, 1952, pp. 86–96.

Khan, Agha, 'The Future of Muslim States in the Background of History', *Pakistan Horizon*, vol. III, no. 1, 1950, pp. 3–8.

———, 'Economic Development in Pakistan and other Muslim States', *Pakistan Horizon*, vol. V, no. 1, 1952, pp. 3–6.

Malik, M.A., 'Pakistan and I.L.O.', *Pakistan Horizon*, vol. VII, no. 2, 1954, pp. 47–56.

Qureshi, I.H., 'The Founder of Pakistan', *Pakistan Horizon*, vol. 1, no. 3, 1948, pp. 144–65.

Rucker, Arthur, 'The Work of International Refugee Organizations', *International Affairs*, vol. XXV, no. 1, 1949, pp. 66–73.

Sayeed, Khalid Bin, 'The Governor-General of Pakistan', *Pakistan Horizon*, vol. VIII, no. 2, 1955, pp. 330–9.

Secretariat Report, 'Some External Aspects of the Economic Problems of Pakistan', *Pakistan Horizon*, vol. VIII, no. 3, 1955, pp. 442–9.

MAGAZINES AND NEWSPAPERS

The Herald (Karachi, monthly).

Newsline (Karachi, monthly).

The Dawn (Karachi).

The News (Karachi).

The Daily Jang (Karachi).

RCSS PUBLICATIONS

- *Defence, Technology and Cooperative Security in South Asia: Report on the Proceedings of the Tenth Summer Workshop* (RCSS, 2004)
- *Environment Development and Human Security: Perspectives from South Asia* (2003)
- *Terrorism in South Asia: Impact on Development and Democratic Process* (SIPRA, 2003)
- *South Asia and the War on Terrorism* (India Research Press, 2003)
- *Shaping the Future–A South Asian Civil Society Dialogue* (RCSS, July 2002)
- *Small Arms and Human Insecurity* (RCSS, July 2002)
- *SAARC in the Twenty-First Century: Towards a Cooperative Future* (July 2002)
- *Memories of a Genocidal Partition: The Haunting Tale of Victims, Witnesses and Perpetrators* (RCSS, July 2002)
- *South Asian Security Futures: A Dialogue of Director's Regional Strategic Studies Institutes* (March 2002)
- *Security and Governance in South Asia* (September 2001)
- *Globalization and Non-Traditional Security in South Asia* (September 2001)
- *Security in the New Millennium* (India Research Press, 2001)
- *The Simla Agreement 1972: Its Wasted Promise* (Manohar, 2001)

RCSS Newsletter

A quarterly bulletin, it publishes a brief report of RCSS activities, presentations at its workshops on topics of contemporary interest and news and programmes of the RCSS and its alumnae.

RCSS Policy Studies

37 Impact of Partition: Refugees in Pakistan (Manohar, 2006)
36 Maritime Cooperation between India and Sri Lanka (Manohar, 2006)
35 Nuclear Risk Reduction Measures in South Asia: Problems and Prospects (Manohar, 2006)
34 Indo-Pak Conflicts: Ripe to Resolve? (Manohar, 2005)
33 Small Arms and the Security Debate in South Asia (Manohar, 2005)
32 New Nuclear Triangle and China's Role in South Asia (RCSS: 2005)
31 Stability through Economic Cooperation in a Nuclear Environment (Manohar, 2005)
30 Multi-Track Diplomacy between India and Pakistan: A Conceptual Framewrok for Sustainable Security (Manohar, 2005)
29 The Role of Mediation in Resolving India-Pakistan Conflict: Parameters and Possibilities (Manohar, 2005)
28 HIV/AIDS as a Security Threat to India (Manohar, 2005)
27 Nepal's Maoist Movement and Implications for India and China (Manohar, 2005)
26 Elite Perceptions in Foreign Policy: Role of Print Media in Influencing India-Pakistan Relations, 1989-1999 (Manohar, 2004)
25 Nuclear Risk Reduction Measures and Restraint Regime in South Asia (Manohar, 2004)
24 River Water Sharing Problem Between India and Pakistan: Case Study of the Indus Basin Water Treaty (June 2004)

Fellowship in South Asian Alternatives (FISAA) Monograph

- Water, Power and People: A South Asian Manifesto on the Politics and Knowledge of Water (1997)
- The Nuclear Debate: Ironies and Immoralities (1998)

Others

- *Directory of Individuals and Institutions Engaged in South Asian Strategic Studies* (1998).